I WELL REMEMBER

A VARIED AND INTERESTING LIFE

PETER NUTTING

To Sara
with love
Peter

CONTENTS

PART III

PART IV

INTRODUCTION

It is extremely pretentious to write a book about one's not very distinguished self. It originates from my children and grandchildren urging me to write down details of my life, particularly when I said, 'I well remember'. I started to do this about four years ago, tapping away on my desktop computer on wet and long winter evenings. When I got to the present, it seemed only practical to ask someone to edit it all. Joanna Booth has done a wonderful job, and here is the finished product. Inevitably, there is much I have left out or friends and associates who are not mentioned. I apologise to them as it is not intentional but rather a result of lapses in my memory.

My father was a very wise and accomplished man and my mother was all one could ever have wanted in a mother. I have been incredibly lucky to have been able to travel widely, shoot,
fish and stalk, sail boats, scuba dive and play cricket, tennis and squash as well as being able to enjoy the company of wonderful friends. At the same time, I have been involved in so many different businesses. It has been a very varied life, which I have thoroughly enjoyed. I could have gone to Cambridge and read law but effectively, I left

school at seventeen. Since then, I have never found the time or had the inclination to get any formal qualifications.

Despite over fifty years in business, I was never a captain of industry and with a few exceptions, I nearly always relied on someone else to manage on a day-to-day basis, the businesses I was involved in. I did not retire from business until well into my seventies and have since then enjoyed our garden and growing vegetables.

The cleverest thing I ever did was marry Poppity. She has great intuition and is a very good judge of people. She has been an exceptional wife, great mother, and wonderful grandmother. She always thinks of others and deserves another medal for putting up with me for fifty-five years.

Peter Robert Nutting

PART I

EARLY DAYS

I was born on 22 October 1935 in the London Clinic. Professor William, later Sir William, Gilliat supervised the delivery. I was about 7 ½ pounds and pretty healthy so I went home to North Breache Manor in Surrey very quickly.

My mother and father had bought North Breache in 1932 for £4750. The house was built in 1873 by the celebrated architect Sir Aston Webb, who designed and built the front of Buckingham Palace in 1913. There were about 110 acres of land; a lodge house; a range of farm buildings, including a large Surrey Barn and a cottage; a stable yard with three garages, formerly coach houses, stabling for a number of horses, a hayloft and a coachman's two-bedroom flat above.

My mother, Patricia Elisabeth, known as Patsy, was thirty when I was born, and my father, Captain Arthur Ronald Stansmore, known as Ronald, was forty-seven. I was christened Peter Robert. My father had served in the Irish Guards for the duration of the First World War and won a Military Cross at the battle of Ypres. He was born in 1888 in Ireland, the youngest son of a very prominent businessman who was also a Dublin senator and a baronet.

He was educated in England at Cheam School and then Eton before going to Cambridge where he got a degree in law. Prior to the war, he worked in the family business E & J Burke, which was the biggest exporter and bottler of Guinness. He also spent some time working for JP Morgan in New York where he met his first wife, Edith Brooks, whose father was the principal shareholder in the Brooks Brothers department store.

After the war, my father took control of the Burke business. His father had died in 1917, leaving a large fortune to his eldest son and very little to his other children. My father was at the front in France whereas his elder brother was aide-de-camp (ADC) to the Duke of Gloucester. Despite being the favourite son, it was thought my father was unlikely to survive the war.

Prohibition in America and Guinness's decision to build a brewery in England badly affected the Burke business. My father, therefore, moved the business into soft drinks by buying the Cantrell and Cochrane (C&C) companies operating in England and Ireland as well as Boston in the USA.

In light of the Guinness connection, my father was invited to become a director of Guinness in 1922 and, a year later, was appointed governor of the Bank of Ireland probably because of his brief banking experience in the USA before the war.

My mother was the eldest daughter of Harry Jameson of the Irish whiskey family and was brought up on the Hill of Howth on the north shore of Dublin Bay. In 1926, aged twenty-one she won the Irish Ladies Golf Championship, beating in succession a number of much older and better-known lady golfers. As a result, she became a bit of a celebrity. My father had a difficult relationship with his wife as she had gone back to America during the war, could not have children and was always sickly except when a party was in the offing. My father had to get a divorce which was not legally possible in Ireland. While doing this he became engaged to my mother and gave her a ring, which she wore on a string around her neck.

Despite having been resident in Ireland most of his life he had actually been born in Birkenhead when his father was briefly working in the Burke office there. With the benefit of weighty legal advice, he was eventually able to get a divorce in England but had to intend to go and live in England after absenting himself from Ireland by effectually going travelling for a year. On his return, he married my mother in London in 1932 and they moved to Surrey.

Unsurprisingly, I have little recollection of my first few years. I vaguely remember travelling to Ireland with my mother by air from Croydon Airport in early 1939 to see my grandparents before my grandfather died. Another early memory was of August 1939. An army car arrived and my father in uniform went away. He had been asked to come out of retirement to be ADC to General, later Field Marshall, Sir John Dill who was to command a corps in the British Expeditionary Force to Belgium and France.

My mother became an air-raid warden. On being notified of an air raid she waved a loud football rattle and on *all clear*, she rang a bell.

At this time, all the servants left except for a silly, young girl called Margaret who had been a housemaid and was clumsy, giggly, and illiterate. Also, our nanny from Wales. Previously we had a butler who was always drunk, a wonderful cook married to him, a senior housemaid, a chauffeur, and a gardener.

We were sent evacuees from the East End of London, I recollect four girls. Three of them were moved very soon but one girl, Pam, stayed on. Having a farm, we were able to eat well, but the evacuees would only eat any meat given to them if they were able to pour copious amounts of vinegar over it. I was told the reason was they had never had meat that was not rotten and vinegar hid the taste,

During the Battle of Britain, in 1940, my brother Nicholas, who was born on 8 July 1937, and I would lie on the lawn where we got a grandstand view of dogfights going on above us in the sky. We were never frightened as, unlike many other children, we were never taken down to the cellar during air raids.

A great sadness was the loss of our lovely nanny. She went back to see her parents in Swansea when there was a huge air raid there. She never returned and my parents were unable to find any news of her. They assumed the whole family were probably killed in the raid.

Nanny was replaced by a governess, Miss MacGeorge, called Sella by us. She was quite elderly and claimed to have a Scottish father but had lived most of her life in Switzerland. My father was sure she was German as she could be heard listening to the radio in German in her room at night. She was a strict disciplinarian and very anti-Nazi. My brother and I were a bit of a joke as we were taken on walks to the village and back in shirts, shorts, and braces. We must have looked pretty ridiculous.

We had lessons with Sella but I learned to read quite early with a cousin of my mother's, Isabella Urquart, who spent a lot of time with us as her husband was away in the army.

By this time, our father was back from France and was working in London as military assistant to the Chief of the Imperial General Staff (CIGS), Field Marshall Sir John Dill. The ADC was Reginald Macdonald-Buchanan who came to stay for many weekends. He was very deaf and had a deaf aid, which he took out at night. On one occasion, there was a terrific bang in the middle of the night as a fleeing German bomber had unloaded its bombs that it had failed to deliver on London. They landed in a wood not far away from the house. We all leapt out of bed and assembled on the landing when someone asked where was Reginald Macdonald-Buchanan? We burst into his bedroom to find him fast asleep covered in broken glass from the window that had been blown in. Clearly, he had not heard a thing.

In 1942, the Americans came into the war and the tide turned so that there was optimism that eventually the Germans would be beaten and we would win. Field Marshall Sir John Dill retired as CIGS and went to Washington to act as a liaison between President Roosevelt and General Marshall on the one hand and Winston Churchill and the new CIGS Sir Alan Brooke. Reginald Macdonald-Buchanan went with him but our father was encouraged to hang up his uniform and retire to work in industry and business. Thereafter, he was always known as Captain Nutting and he received a military OBE to go with his MC.

North Breache had a chestnut and lime avenue, leading from the gate and the lodge up to the house, and for half the length of the drive, there was a three-or-four-acre wood. Early on in the war, the lodge was requisitioned by the army and a fuel depot was established in the wood. Lorries were parked on the side of the drive. Towards the end of the war, there was an ugly incident. Military petrol was dyed red. Our father had a small car and a small petrol ration to enable him to get to work. Spot checks were carried out to see that red military petrol was not being stolen. One such check found that our father's car had red petrol in it and he was accused of stealing military petrol. Things looked very serious until it was discovered that all the local car owners were equally guilty as the local garage had been given a delivery of red petrol by mistake.

SCHOOL

$\mathcal{T}$he war was still going on when it was decided I should go to boarding school. It was my father's old school, Cheam, now in a splendid building near Newbury in Berkshire. I went in May 1944 aged eight. I was a slightly sickly child prone to upset tummies or bilious attacks as they were termed. Unfortunately, I was suffering from such an attack and so I was three days late arriving. I had no idea what to expect. The first thing I remember was the matron taking my small teddy bear from me rather roughly and saying, 'We don't have that sort of thing here.' I don't think I cried!

The next memory is of going into my first class, which was Latin. I had never heard of Latin and was absolutely baffled by *amo, I love*, etc. There were seventy boys in the school and I was in a class of about fourteen. The headmaster was Rev HMS Taylor. He and his wife were pillars of Moral Rearmament or Buckmanism. It was a sort of born-again Christianity but was regarded with a lot of suspicion as an American import. The school had extensive grounds and owned a large patch of woodland where we were allowed to play, build camps, and do Cubs and Scouts activities.

It being the summer, we all had to learn to swim. There was a large swimming pool but no filtration, chlorine, or heating. The pool was filled, which took a few days. We were given swimming lessons with a master who had a stout stick with a line to a bicycle tyre that went around our tummies. The whole school swam and splashed around for a bit over a week until the water went green and became like soup. They'd then use a fire pump to empty the pool into a shrubbery. It was then scrubbed and cleaned before being refilled.

In addition to the headmaster, the rest of the staff were a strange bunch with the benefit of hindsight. They were either old like Mr Davies, fat like Mr Sims, or had something wrong with them like Mr Malden. I don't recollect any of them being married. Mr Anderson was very tall and was clearly having an affair with the lady who taught music. They were seen kissing through the music room window.

Mr Anderson was the Scoutmaster and he had rather odd ideas of punishment for bad work. We were made to stand on our desks and lower our shorts and underpants. We thought this very funny but it could not happen today and undoubtedly should not have happened then. Another strange idea was that a master patrolled the school lavatories after breakfast where there were no doors on the cubicles.

At my first half term, my parents struggled to get to the school by train, which took many hours as a V2 bomb landed on the line somewhere and the damage had to be repaired before the train could proceed.

A lasting memory was D-Day in June. Greenham Common was an American airbase and was just to the north of the school. We were awakened at daybreak by a stream of DC3s towing gliders, flying over the school. This went on nearly all day. The gliders, which each carried about twenty soldiers and their equipment, were towed across the Channel and then let go to land where they could in France, behind enemy lines.

I was very young and felt fairly homesick much of the time. For most of my time at Cheam, I hated going back to school but got into the routine when I got there. I did not find the work difficult and exams easier so after a slow start I was in the top stream for most subjects.

We played cricket in the summer, which I enjoyed, doing a bit of batting and bowling. Soccer and rugby in the winter terms. We were not very good at any sport and on one occasion we played a match against Horris Hill, a much larger school. I was the first-team goalkeeper. Horris Hill kicked eleven goals past me and so, I gave up goalkeeping and soccer. I think I preferred rugby, and I was due to captain the rugby team in my last Lent term. Sadly, it snowed everywhere soon after Christmas and the snow and frozen ground lasted until the end of term, so we played no rugby at all. This was the famous winter of 1947 when the whole country closed down, the Thames froze over, and there were extensive power cuts. There has never been a repeat.

In the summer, a highlight was a visit by Princess Elizabeth and her fiancé, Prince Philip of Greece, later the Queen and Prince Philip. He was an old boy of the school. We were given a holiday.

Of course, the food was pretty awful. We got a large slice of bread covered in dripping at the mid-morning break, which I could not eat. At least twice each week, we got a Telfers Meat pie for lunch. What went into these was a mystery but one day, a boy found what could only have been the tail of a rat.

In the summer of 1948, it was time for the Common Entrance exam to Eton. I passed into Upper Fourth, which was very respectable. Everybody was very pleased as I was still only twelve years old.

ETON

I arrived at Eton in September 1948, just before my thirteenth birthday. I was in bum freezers as I was not tall enough to wear tails. This consisted of a mess type black jacket, striped trousers, and a large white collar over the jacket, and a black straight tie. My first-form master was Rev Gordon Taylor who later became Rector of St Martin's in the Fields in Trafalgar Square.

My housemaster was CRN Routh and our house overlooked Sixpenny. It was called the Timbralls and was one of the better houses. CRNR was a confirmed bachelor, bald, a good historian, and ran a very good house. He taught history. He was in his last year before retiring from having a house. We had a room of our own, which was a very new experience. It looked out over the yard of Drill Hall Schools. We had early school at 7.30 am, which involved walking to wherever the classroom was. This lasted forty minutes and we then returned to our houses for breakfast. Then there was chapel, followed by a number of classes before lunch back in the house with the approximately forty-five other boys in the house. It was more classes after lunch, except Wednesdays and Saturdays when we played sport, which was taken very seriously.

In my first Michaelmas term, it was the Field Game. This was a hybrid version of soccer and rugby unique to Eton, the rules of which I won't try to explain. Suffice it to say, it was a marvellous game, which I was quite good at and enjoyed through all my time at Eton.

We seldom saw CRNR except when he came to say goodnight to us.

Our lives were run by the senior boys in the house who we fagged for. The captain of the house had the right to cane us and did so for any offence. Members of the Library, the house prefects, had the right to shout 'Boy!' at which all lower boys (first two years) had to run to wherever they were. The last to arrive was given the errand, which probably involved taking a note to another boy in another house. To fail to answer the call was a sure way of being beaten.

At about 5 pm each day, we had tea in one of our rooms. Typically, three of us would join up and eat in one of our rooms. During my time at Eton, I messed, as it was called, with Simon Horn, Ranulf Rayner, Charles Owen, Paul Irby and Nick Calvert. All have remained friends many years later. We brought from home or bought in Rowlands in the High Street all manner of food. There were cooking facilities available and sometimes someone would, for example, bring a pheasant which could be plucked and cooked at Rowlands.

All rooms had open fireplaces and we were given a coal ration and kindling so we could have a fire on which to make toast and keep us warm because the central heating was pretty limited or non-existent. After tea, there was lock-up at 6.30 pm where we had to stay in our rooms until 8 pm, doing work that would have been set earlier in the day. After lock-up, there was supper in the house dining room followed by free time before bed around 10 pm.

All lower boys had to fag for older boys to whom one was allotted. My first fag master was Patrick Drury Lowe who lived a rich and rare life at home and was most demanding. I had to put his bed down (the beds lifted up behind a curtain by day to give more room), lay out his pyjamas and slippers, and tidy his room.

Shoes were cleaned centrally by Ginger who tended the hot water boiler and was the janitor. There was a boys' maid on each of three floors, who made our beds and swept the floor. She also helped with the arrangements for tea, looking after the plates knives and forks etc.

In each house, there was a Dame, a sort of matron, so-called, who looked after our health and helped run the house, meals, etc. The food was not good but better than some as CRNR subsidised it out of his own money.

After a year at the Timbralls, it was all change. I graduated into a tailcoat and neat white tie. CRNR retired and was replaced by WW Williams, and so we had to move house to Carter House in Keats Lane by College Chapel. This was a very old building where the rooms and everything else was a big step down from the Timbralls.

WWW, Watcyn Wynne Williams known as Fishy due to him having a bit of a lisp, was a slightly comic character. He was again another bachelor but he lived with his sister and mother. The former was as thin as a stick and was obviously what we now know as anorexic. The latter was a peculiarly unattractive old woman who spent much of her time in a wheelchair. The sister was known by us as Death because that is what she looked like.

He had a large moustache and was a very senior member of the Scouting movement. He was also very naïve and considerable advantage was taken of this.

A year later, I became an Upper Boy and there was a great shock when my brother was told the house he was entered for had no room for him. My father came down to Eton and asked Fishy what could be done and could he help. Fishy said he would but the condition was we should share a room so long as we were both together at the school. So, we were given a senior boy's room, which we shared for a year in Carter House.

After two years in Carter House, we moved to Baldwins Bec, a much nicer building near the top of Eton High Street at the back of College Chapel. We still had to share a room but this was a big room overlooking College Chapel graveyard.

I was enjoying cricket in the summer and was in the house-side with mainly older boys. It was Field Game before Christmas and then I elected to play squash and fives in the Lent term.

In the summer, it was School Certificate.

A year previously, we were divided into Greekas and Kappas. The former were the top third and the latter the remainder. I was a Greeka and so I was going to do Greek as well as Latin for School Certificate, where I think I did quite well.

In year four, it was time to specialise, and I decided to do history, maths and French. We were then allotted a tutor who would be in charge of our academic progress. I found myself with Mr Barker who did not take to me, and I did not take to him. He used to accuse me of being long-winded and pompous, which I probably was but he nearly put me off history. I think he left Eton shortly after me and became headmaster of the Leys School at Cambridge. He also married the famous Lady Trumpington

Every boy had to do an item of exercise each day or five days a week and this was recorded on a board. In most houses, the house-master was hugely involved in encouraging boys to be good at something and the house team to be winners in everything. He would make sure the senior boys and the house captain also worked hard in this direction. In a number of cases, house masters used to visit prep schools, find out who the outstanding athletes, cricketers etc., were, and offer places in their houses. WWW was the exception. He was not interested, and the net result was we were always very bad at sport.

I got no encouragement when I wanted to organise a house cricket side and the various football house sides were invariably knocked out in the first round of the house competitions. We had some individual stars. Christopher Clogg was a very good footballer and Simon Horn set a new record for the mile in athletics.

I was a competent cricketer and played in Strawberry Mess and effectively provided the 3rd XI. I was given my house colours for the Field Game at a time when our house was only allowed three capped people because of our dismal performance in the house competition. I just failed to get a cap for squash and tennis, which was a bit disappointing.

AWAY FROM SCHOOL

I loved home and spent a lot of time working in the garden
and on the farm. For part of the summer, we'd go to Ireland
and stay with our grandmother at Drumleck on the Hill of Howth,
overlooking Dublin Bay. There, we'd see many relations, eat wonderful
food, and play a lot of tennis. When I was sixteen, I used to make up a
four with my cousins, Shane Jameson and Patrick Jameson, and Guy
Jackson who was the No 1 Davis Cup player for Ireland.

One summer, I played in the Cranleigh tennis tournament and got
into the semi-finals of the Under-18 boys. There, I came up against Reg
Bennet, who later had a successful career as a tennis player and was
badly beaten. However, I received an invitation to compete in Junior
Wimbledon that next July 1953. That was not to be as it clashed with
the end of term examinations, which were to be sent to Cambridge for
marking to determine whether I had scored well enough to go there
for university. I did, however, enter the Cranleigh tennis tournament
again the following year. After victory in one round, I came up against
Bobby Wilson, a future Wimbledon singles semi-finalist. I was more-
or-less annihilated but I did get one game off him by serving three
aces.

In 1951 and 1952, we did summer holidays in the west of Ireland. My father took a house at Ballyconneely near Clifden. It had a lovely beach and rocks where we looked for and found lobsters and crabs and some bogs where we shot some snipe. There was one big store in Clifden owned by Eddie King who would dress in striped pants, a black jacket, and waistcoat with a large watch chain. On being introduced to him, he ruffled my hair, which I hated and said, 'If ever there was a boy who was blessed; his father a director of Guinness and his mother a Jameson.' I guess they were two of his best-selling products but, of course, my father was well-known in Ireland.

The house at Ballyconneely was pretty primitive and had a diesel generator to provide electricity. I was told how to start it, which was to give it two big hits with a hammer that was provided and then wind the handle. This invariably worked. Another feature was the milk. Before breakfast, either I or my brother went on a bicycle to a small-holding about half a mile from the house. The lady took us out to a cow behind the cottage. There she proceeded to milk the cow into a funnel in a cider bottle with a spring-loaded cap. When filled, we'd take the warm milk back and put it on our cereal.

Thinking of this brings me back to the cow we had at home during the war. Apart from the herd of Red Poles, we had a Guernsey cow called Mary who produced lovely creamy milk, which would be given to me and my brother. At the end of the war, testing for tuberculosis was introduced for all dairy cows. Mary was found to be riddled with TB and had to immediately be destroyed. I think we probably have a strong immunity to TB.

The following year, we took another house not far away in the west of Ireland. It had a lake by the house, which produced some trout. The highlight was the existence of some grouse. My brother and I walked miles over heather and bog, and we successfully shot a few grouse.

My father loved fishing and would spend many hours just casting into a loch, usually with little success. We paid to go fishing on a quite well-known fishery where we fished from a boat for salmon with no luck much to father's disappointment. Sometime later, the owner of the fishery was arrested and charged with theft because people had paid to fish for salmon when he had netted the entrance to the river so no salmon could get up it.

After five years at Eton, I felt it was time to leave in the summer of 1953. I was four months short of eighteen and I could have stayed on for another year and become very grand but another year with Fishy Williams was a turn-off.

GROWN-UP AND IN THE ARMY

*H*aving left Eton, I looked back on my career there and it was spectacularly undistinguished. As a house, we were not good at anything although there were the odd individual performers. I did not have a wide circle of friends or an active social life in the holidays. My parents led a very quiet life with my father still working hard in not very good health. Sure, I had good friends in my house who are still friends as I write this and lots of acquaintances who came into one's life later. Eton was a very good club.

Two years previously, Charles Owen and I had gone on a week's skiing trip with a school party to Arosa. We went by train. I fell madly in love with a red-headed girl but she was not much interested in me. I enjoyed skiing but always found it difficult to stop or turn. It was fifteen years until I tried skiing again.

National Service was the next step. At Eton, I had been interviewed by Colonel (later Brigadier) Fitzgerald and had been told that subject to passing everything, a commission in the Irish Guards was probable. This had as much to do with me as to a massive regimental connection. My father had served in both World Wars as had my uncle and numerous cousins.

I would not be eighteen until the end of October so could not be called up until then.

We had some friends who lived in Paris and they said they would look after me for a month in France. They, in turn, had friends who lived on the Loire in Western France and would be happy to have me as a paying guest and would talk French with me.

Cecile and Regis Courtemanche had a farm near Cour Cheverny in the centre of the Chateaux of the Loire. He was a red-faced pipe smoker and she was quite vivacious. I cycled a lot on my own but also with a girl of my age from the next farm. Cecile also took me by car to see a number of chateaux. It was an amusing month, my French improved but I was happy to return home.

Next, I had to get my driving test. I failed twice. First, because I was not good enough and second, because I went round a roundabout the wrong way. I then passed.

Then in early October, I had to go to Cambridge to see the Master of Trinity Hall, my father's old college. Henry Dean was a distinguished pathologist and after interviewing me, he said that my results in the final trials/exams, where I had got a first class, persuaded him to offer me a place once I had completed national service. It was even agreed that I should probably read law like my father.

Then, suddenly, I got my call-up papers about a week before my birthday. This was a mistake as they probably read '12' instead of '22' as the date of my birthday. My mother drove me to the rather grim gates of the Guards Depot at Caterham. I was in the Brigade Squad of potential officers commanded by Captain Ian Erskine with a squad sergeant, Ray Huggins, a grenadier who many years later was the academy sergeant major at Sandhurst. There were about twenty of us in a hut/barrack room. My fellow Irish Guards were Peter Verney, who had already been to university, Trinity Dublin; Robin Bonham Carter who was 6ft 4in and a very good sportsman. He had been to Clifton College and captained the rest against the public schools at cricket in the match at Lords. He was also destined to play rugby for the army. Lastly, there was Patrick Alexander who was a contemporary at Eton and was a nephew of the field marshal.

The next eight weeks were drill, more drill, being shouted at, virtually running everywhere, and polishing one's boots and brasses. To press our trousers, we damped them and then slept on them. There was very limited hot water and the only heating was a stove, which we filled with coke and wood.

A highlight was a boxing night. On being asked whether we boxed, most of us kept quiet but Robin Dixon (later Lord Glentoran) put his hand up. He was selected to fight a sergeant in the grenadiers who was much bigger and heavier than him and was an army champion. The said-sergeant chased Robin around the ring for three rounds but such was Robin's skill that hardly a worthwhile punch was landed on him.

After eight weeks, we passed out from Caterham and were sent to Pirbright where we fired rifles and did military exercises. We also learned to throw hand grenades. You take the pin out and throw it from a dugout. The member of the squad in front of me took the pin out and dropped it at my feet. My reaction was to pick it up and throw it, which I did. This got me into trouble as we had been told the right thing to do was to immediately go around the corner in the dugout and let it explode.

Another amusing incident occurred when we were on a parade and being inspected by the regimental sergeant major, Dusty Smith of the Coldstream Guards

He came to James Haywood Lonsdale, looked him up and down, and asked, 'Do you read the Bible?'

James stuttered, 'Yes.'

The reply was, 'Then you will know what it says in Psalm 95, otherwise known as The Venite, Verse 4; In his hands he all the four corners of the earth.' Then he exploded, 'And you, you, horrible man, sir, have got them under your fingernails!'

We all burst out laughing but that was military humour.

Sadly, Heywood Lonsdale was the only member of our squad who failed the War Office Selection Board (WOSB), which involved a visit to Barton Stacey for two days while we each gave a ten-minute lecture, did intelligence tests, and, in turn, organised team events like crossing a ditch with a number of items, which on their own were not long enough.

After Pirbright, we passed out and prepared to become officer cadets at Eaton Hall in Cheshire. As a finale to our basic training, I was tasked with organising a dinner for the squad and instructors. We had a private room in the Angel Hotel in Guildford, which was a Trust House hotel. It helped that my father was chairman of Trust Houses.

Eaton Hall OTC was a huge Victorian house leased from the Duke of Westminster with numerous huts in the grounds where we lived. Our instructors consisted of a Welsh Guards Company sergeant major and a captain in the Greenjackets. The commandant was Colonel White who appears again in this chronicle in Dominica. I was separated from those in my squad at Caterham and Pirbright and found myself in a hut of about twenty with only three others destined for the Guards.

Once again, we needed to avoid the regimental sergeant major, an Irish Guardsman, Benny Lynch, who could be terrifying.

Day-to-day training to be an officer was pretty mundane but we had two trips to do battle training. The first was to Okehampton on Dartmoor. I had agreed with Robin Bonham Carter and Patrick Alexander to share the costs of running a 1937 Vauxhall, which Robin had acquired. We were allowed to drive to Okehampton in it where we found a considerable amount of snow. The battle training was tough and very cold but one evening we were able to go into Okehampton in our car about ten miles away from the camp.

All was well until the car stopped on the way back. We opened the bonnet and the plugs were glowing white-hot and the engine block was a dull red. It seems that somewhere along the way the sump had come off. We had to get back to camp and were lucky to get a lift. We removed the tax disc and number plates and anything that would identify us as the owners and left the Vauxhall by the side of the road. That was the end of my first car.

One notable occupant of our hut was the later well-known actor Jeremy Kemp. My friends in the hut were Ian Bowater, who had been at Eton with me, and Philip Ashworth. The latter had a degree and was destined for the Education Corp. He became our under officer in due course. Another friend was Guy Knott who was in the squad at Caterham, etc. and was destined for the Life Guards. He and I used to go into Chester and have a good meal and some good wine. He was not accepted by the Life Guards and I believe later changed his name to Mansell. During our training, we did get to London from time to time and Guy was a member of the long-closed Public Schools Club in Piccadilly just West of the In and Out. I joined and it was a good base for a short length of time. Guy Knott/Mansell was a good friend at that time but he did his time in West Africa and I never saw him again.

After a very uncomfortable week at Trosfinith in the Welsh Mountains, doing more battle training, we were ready to pass out as officers. There were about 120 of us and Robin Bonham Carter won the Sword of Honour and was the senior under officer for the parade.

It was the end of May, and I was now a 2nd lieutenant in the Irish Guards aged eighteen. I could have still been at Eton if I had stayed on.

After a short break, I went to regimental headquarters in Wellington Barracks where I drew my officers kit, which included khaki drill tropical uniform as I was due to fly to Egypt in a very short time and join the battalion. This was put in a tin trunk and send out ahead of me.

In early June, I reported at Goodge Street in London from where I found myself at an airport, embarking in an Avro York. This was a so-called civilian version of a Lancaster bomber. It was incredibly noisy. I was with Robin B-C, Patrick Alexander and Peter Verney. We landed to refuel in the south of France, near Rome, and then Tripoli and then to an airfield near the Suez Canal. The Irish Guards were at Berwick Camp near Fanara, which was about half a mile from the Great Bitter Lake through which runs the Suez Canal. It was very hot as it was midsummer. I found myself sharing a tent with John Maclean who had joined the battalion three months earlier. The tent had two beds, two chests of drawers, as well as a writing desk and a rail to hang one's clothes on and was on a concrete base.

The officers' mess was a brick-and-block building and was quite comfortable. The regiment had a strange custom that nobody spoke to newly joined officers for about a month or so and so we kept our own company. The first thaw in this was an invitation to join the poker school, which I did. This was run by the second in command, Mick O'Cock, and the stakes and what was lost were closely monitored.

We were on active service, performed guard duties, and went out on patrols. We were regarded by the Egyptians as an occupying force, which they wished to get rid of. Where we could go while off duty, was strictly limited. The Egyptians were unfriendly and took the odd pot shot at us. Thus, we were confined to the mess inside the camp most evenings.

I recollect there was a party one night in the sergeants' mess about two weeks after our arrival. The officers were all invited, and the objective was to get them drunk. I had had quite a few drinks given to me and must have been swaying a bit as the regimental quartermaster, Sergeant Jimmy Kelly, saw me, grabbed me by the arm, and said he thought I needed a bit of fresh air. I went outside with him and promptly threw up. He suggested I went back to my tent, which I did.

I was always grateful to him for that act of kindness as, otherwise, I would probably have thrown up in the sergeants' mess itself. I was, after all, only a bit over 18 ½ years old and, looking back, I'd had a very sheltered life and was very green behind the ears.

I was in No 4 Company as a platoon officer, commanding some twenty-four Guardsmen. Life was rather monotonous. We went to the officers' club on the banks of the Great Bitter Lake where we swam and played tennis. In the evenings, I moved from the poker game to bridge where the priest, Father Quinlan, held sway. He claimed he had played bridge for Ireland and to my certain knowledge he never paid a mess bill as his bridge winnings were credited to his account each month. Anyhow, the stakes were not high, and I learned to be quite a good bridge player.

In December, Robin Bonham Carter and I were called into the adjutant's office and told we were to fly to Akaba where an Irish Guards company commanded by Major Mark White was stationed. We were to collect two Land Rovers and drive them up to Amman. There, they would be used by the major general commanding London District who was visiting Guards regiments in the Middle East.

The following day, we flew in a Viking cargo plane. It had no seats so we sat on the floor with all the doors open over the Sinai desert to Akaba. We were welcomed by the company there and told there would be a reception and dinner that evening given by the local chief, the Mukta of Akaba. Thereafter, Mark White was nicknamed the Mukta. Dinner was a mixture of vegetables and goat, which was perfectly good but the highlight was Mark White being offered the eye of the sheep on a fork, which he reluctantly swallowed

The next day, we collected our Land Rovers and drivers, a guardsman, and a lance sergeant and set off to drive north. It was steep uphill on dirt roads to our first stop near Petra. This was an Arab Legion fort, painted white and with a gate enclosing a yard where they fed us and we bedded down for the night. This was true Lawrence of Arabia country. There were spectacular desert landscapes.

After a night's sleep and some breakfast, it was suggested we visited some Petra ruins. We just drove in in the Land Rovers until it was too narrow. We were the only people there in this famous place that is now covered in hotels and tourists.

Next, we drove on to Kerak, a huge crusader castle and the HQ of the Arab Legion Camel Corps. There were around 200 camels in stalls and all beautifully groomed. The castle was used as barracks and so we were housed in the officers' mess for the night and our drivers were equally well looked after.

The next day, we drove to Amman and reported to Colonel Buster Luard, who was chief of staff to General Glubb – Glubb Pasha, as he was known. Both were British officers on secondment to the Kingdom of Transjordan. Buster Luard told us he had excellent news for us. The major general would not be coming as there was some problem he had to sort out at home. He had been in touch with our commanding officer in Fanara who had said we could have a week's leave and we could take the vehicles to Jerusalem. He said, 'Go and get a night's sleep in the Arab Legion mess and come and report to me here in the morning.'

In the morning, we duly reported back only to be asked whether we wanted the good news or the bad news first. He told us he had received a signal from our commanding officer that we were wanted back at the battalion and we should promptly leave for the return trip to Akaba. Crestfallen, we asked what was the good news. He said he had only received the signal minutes ago and suggested he reply by saying we had already departed to Jerusalem and he would not see us again for a week. 'Go on. Bugger off and enjoy yourselves,' he said, and we left thinking he was the nicest man in the world.

This was 1954 and all the places of interest in Jerusalem were in Transjordan. We drove down over the River Jordan and on to Jerusalem. We found a lovely small hotel on a hill just outside the city walls. From there, we could see the Dome of the Rock and the Garden of Gethsemane. We let the drivers take one of the vehicles and we kept the other in the small car park beside the hotel.

It is no exaggeration to say there were hardly any tourists. We spent five fantastic days looking at everything, including the Wailing Wall, the Church of the Holy Sepulchre, the Dome, and the Garden of Gethsemane as well as Golgotha. We talked with an Irish Priest who tended the garden and looked after the church at Gethsemane. Many of the olive trees were 2000 years old and would have been there when Jesus was. One day, we took the car to Bethlehem, where I recollect the birthplace of Christ was very simple. Nowadays, I believe there is a big church there.

To have visited at that time with total freedom to go where we wished and with no whiff of tourism was a unique experience.

On our way back to Amman, we deviated to the Dead Sea, which is below sea level and super salty. We swam but so salty was the water that it was difficult to stay upright. We reported to Buster Luard's office but he was not there and so we set off back to Akaba. Near Petra, it started to snow and so, we spent a night with our Arab Legion friends and set off again in about 4 inches of snow, which stopped and died out as we went down to Akaba.

Our return to the battalion was accompanied by some incredulity that we had not received that signal!

It was back to being picket officer, inspecting sentries, overseeing meals, and confined to camp. One evening, just before supper, there was a loud bang from the orderly room tent, which was the centre of operations and included the commanding officer's and adjutant's offices. One of the clerks had put a rifle in his mouth and blown the top off his head. The picket sergeant and I ran to the tent whereupon the sergeant fainted. We raised the alarm and I started to clear up the horrible mess with a dustpan and brush, which was all I could find. Someone took over from me, and I went outside and was sick. The poor man had just heard his wife had left him

Soon, it was Christmas and then we were told we would be moving camp to Ismailia, further up the canal. There was also talk of a peace treaty with the Egyptians, which would allow us much greater freedom to travel in the country.

Connaught Camp Moasca consisted of many more permanent buildings and was on the edge of Ismailia, a substantial town. We lived in the same tents, and this time I shared with Michael Spring Rice who had just arrived. We became very great and lasting friends.

In February, I was sent back to England to do an assault-pioneer course with the Royal Engineers near Chatham. This lasted four weeks at the end of which, I knew all about blowing things up and building bridges and latrines. I got the weekends off, which was nice as I could go home.

Then I was back to Moasca by air again where I was told that in addition to commanding the assault-pioneer platoon in Support Company, I was to be put in charge of the officers' mess, reporting to the second in command, Stephen Langton. To this end, the mess sergeant, Mulrennan, and I were sent to the Army Pay Corps who ran a week-long course in accounting and double-entry bookkeeping. We both found this very easy and I got 100% in the final exam. I was told I was the first officer to get an A on a course in living memory... rather shameful.

I took over running the mess and continued to do so until I left the army. Michael Boyle, of whom much more later, was the previous PMC as it was called and the finances were in a mess. My instruction was to sort things out, which I did, and this was certainly the first of many businesses I have run. Sergeant Mulrennan had also got an A on the course and proved very efficient.

A breakthrough happened when we caught the master cook, Lt. Sergeant Wilson, taking a backhander from the principal supplier of meat and vegetables. A bonus arrangement and threats that any further backhanders would result in going back to the battalion cookhouse resulted in at least a 10% reduction in food costs.

In addition to running the officers' mess, I was Intelligence Officer for six months and I was also Fire Officer, which had involved going on a course to learn about firefighting. These were all part-time jobs but it meant I was not involved in the day-to-day tedium of being a company officer commanding a platoon.

There were many amusing incidents. Desmond Lambert was a major from rural Ireland where he had a substantial property. He had a soldier servant who had been his butler/driver. Major David Frazer, later General Sir David, known as the Razor was a very serious soldier. One night he was delayed and went and slept in Desmond Lambert's tent as Desmond was away. In the morning, Major Frazer was roughly awakened by the soldier servant unaware of the change of masters.

'Will you be having tea or brandy and soda?' he asked.

The Razor was furious at the suggestion he might need brandy.

On another night, in the mess, we entertained the officers of a USA warship that was passing through the canal. The US Navy was dry and so the entire crew of officers got hopelessly drunk and had to be carried back on board their ship.

My cousin, Anthony Nutting, as minister of state at the Foreign Office, had visited Egypt and signed a treaty with Colonel Nasser whereby we were friends again and would in a few months' time start withdrawing all our troops from Egypt. This meant we could visit Cairo and Alexandria and even go to Upper Egypt to visit Luxor.

I had been playing quite a lot of cricket for a household brigade team. We were now able to go and play against the Gezira Club and also to Alexandria. There, we were entertained by Fares Sarofim, a leading businessman who was a member of the MCC. Staying in his house one night in a huge bed on a platform, I was woken by a rumble and shaking and my bed tipped off the platform. We rushed out of our rooms but were assured all was well. By contrast, a number of not-so-well-built buildings in the area had collapsed. That was my first experience of an earthquake.

Another pleasure was a rest camp that we had set up south of Suez on the Gulf of Suez. Here, companies were taken for R&R, swimming, and a bit of training. There was a reef, which teemed with fish and was excellent for snorkelling. This was not improved as the time came for us to leave Egypt, as we found a grenade dropped on the reef produced a lot of eatable fish.

I also recollect there was a natural feature in the rocks about a mile from the camp adjacent to the road, south, where an outcrop looked a bit like the head of the Sphinx. I thought the assault-pioneer platoon needed some training and so we laid a ring of explosive charges and with an almighty bang, the feature totally disappeared.

In October, as my national service was coming to an end, I contacted Cambridge and told them I would not be coming next year as I had decided to stay on in the army.

In February 1956, the whole battalion embarked on SS Lancashire in Port Said for the journey home. This was a really grotty old troop-ship. Senior officers got a cabin of their own and juniors shared. Guardsmen were on troop decks with cots three high one above another. Many Guardsmen had been flown out to Egypt and had never been on a ship. They were immediately sick and so the stench from the troop decks became increasingly bad, particularly when we ran into very severe gales off Portugal. So severe was the weather that we over-took the Queen Mary, which was virtually hove to.

Inspecting the troop decks became agonising but how much worse for the wretched Guardsmen. The officers' mess in the wardroom had a piano, and I recollect being entertained by Shane Rideau, the field marshal's son, who had the ability to play virtually anything despite not reading music.

We arrived in Dover and moved not far away to Lydd Camp near Rye in Kent. This was a traditional brick-built barracks and the regime was going to be boring as we were perfecting our drill preparatory to going to Wellington Barracks in London. By now, I was a lieutenant with two pips, having served for two years.

We had some leave, which I used in part to buy a car. It was a second-hand black XK 120 Jaguar with two seats and a soft top. It cost £300. I had saved a bit of money from my allowance rather than my net pay, which was around £30 per month.

I found I was on some sort of list and invitations started to arrive to dances and cocktail parties from people I had never heard of. Lydd was some 85 miles from London but we thought nothing of driving to London for these parties and then driving back again much later. We used to rendezvous at the Guards Club in Charles Street at about 4 am and then race back to Lydd. There were no motorways and so we went all through south London, Swanley, Maidstone, and Ashford. There were hardly any dual carriageways. Of course, we had been drinking. I never managed to break the hour for this journey but a Welsh Guards Officer did but he had a Jaguar XK 140, a newer model than mine.

One of the nice things about our 3 months in Lydd was its proximity to Rye Golf Course. Colin Clive was a good friend who had been at Eton a year behind me and had just joined the battalion. He had been brought up on a golf course and played off four or five. The two of us were welcomed by the Secretary of Rye and played this wonderful course at least three times a week. We did our drill parades in the morning and went off to Rye as soon as possible. There we played eighteen holes and then drove to London for the next party.

All this golf and playing with Colin regularly reduced my handicap to ten, which is the lowest it has ever been. After about two months, we were invited to become members; no entrance fee and £5 per year.

I also continued to play cricket and in June went out to Germany to play for the Guards against a team of Guards stationed near Dusseldorf. I don't remember the result but the aftermath was eventful. A number of us drove into the city, did the round of the bars, and then went to the red-light district. Here were situated three houses adjacent to each other. One catered for private soldiers, another for non-commissioned officers, and the best one for officers. A number of us went into the officers' establishment where about ten girls with a limited amount of clothing sat in a row. We behaved rather badly and the Madame decided we should leave with threats of calling the police.

As we departed, a fellow Irish Guards officer who was with us thrust a thunder flash through the letterbox. It went off with a huge bang and shattered some glass in the door. Almost immediately, police cars and policemen were everywhere. Three of us ran for it and got away but others were arrested and taken back to the police station. When it was discovered they were British Army officers, the police were powerless to do anything and they had to be released.

About a year later, after he had left the army, my brother was not quite so lucky. He and some friends had the idea of dealing with the numerous ladies of the night who stood on Park Lane touting for business. While one drove the car and stopped to talk to one of the ladies, the other lay on the floor with a soda water syphon and squirted the lady in the face while the driver drove off. They tried this rather unkind trick once too often and were stopped by police and arrested for insulting behaviour. Happily, the police saw the funny side, regarded the ladies as a nuisance, and released them after a night in the cells.

In July, it was time to move to London. I was sufficiently senior to be allowed to live out in a flat in London. Michael Boyle suggested I joined him and Jeremy Durham Matthews in a flat he had found to rent in Wellington Court in Knightsbridge. It was an ancient mansion block. We had a drawing-room, a dining room, three bedrooms and three bathrooms, together with a large kitchen. There was staff accommodation at the top of the building and we arranged for each of our three soldier servants to be able to stay over.

Jeremy's man was called Finnegan, and he had been valet to the British Ambassador in Dublin. Michael's was Hamilton and he stayed on with him after he'd left the army and became his butler/chauffeur. I had a rather dozy fellow called Wood. They looked after all our kit, which was quite considerable, doing public duties in London.

Militarily, it was a fairly repetitious programme of Tower Guard, which involved doing the Ceremony of the Keys at 10 pm and staying in the Fusilier Mess overnight. Mostly however it was guard mounting outside Buckingham Palace, marching to St James's Palace where there was an officers' mess where we could entertain guests for lunch, drinks, and dinner. At intervals, we had to go and inspect the sentries at St James's Palace and I usually had to march up to Buckingham Palace in full uniform, inspect the sentries outside and then into the garden where there were more sentries. I did this with the guard sergeant and then we'd march back again. Entertaining on guard was a great way of returning hospitality and very popular with girls.

I gave up running the officers' mess and the assault pioneers and was appointed assistant transport officer. This was not very onerous but one of my jobs was to act as a driving examiner for Guardsmen who wanted to pass the army's driving test, which could immediately be exchanged for a full-civilian driving licence. I recollect some very hairy moments being driven around Trafalgar Square by really bad drivers. I think I was very strict on who I would pass and who not as I had visions of someone I had passed mowing down a bus queue.

MY FIRST GIRLFRIEND AND SOME
SOCIALISING

*I*n the summer, I acquired my first serious girlfriend. Dawn Kettlewell was the daughter of our previous family GP and who was now living in Oxford. There she shared a flat with a girlfriend. I am ashamed to say my brother had invited her to lunch at home at North Breache. I gave her a lift back to London and it started from there. I was still, however, going out with other girls when Dawn was not around.

My social life was blossoming. Michael Boyle, who had been left a large house in Hampshire and quite a lot of money when his mother died, entertained in a grand manner. London was one round of parties and a lot of them were at Wellington Court.

Directly below us – we were on the third floor – was the Wellington Club, which was not a pick-up joint but rather a quiet dining and night club run by Mr and Mrs Victor Ledger. The doorman was quite well-known and was called Ginger. He was a great friend and so when we'd run out of gin or tonic or anything else, we used to open the window, lower a basket on a rope and shout to Ginger, 'Bottle of Gordons and a dozen tonic!' He'd duly fill the basket and we'd haul it up.

We also patronised the 400 in Leicester Square and the Café de

Paris. It was at the latter, one night when they apologised that Eartha Kitt was unwell but they had a worthy replacement for the first time in London, Miss Shirley Bassey. She was amazing with a wonderfully powerful voice that was commented on in the papers the following day.

One evening, we had a parents' dinner party cooked by a lady, Mrs Barkley – who had fallen on hard times. It was served up by our soldier servants who waited on us at the table. Commander Boyle was a very retired navy man, and Rita, Michael's stepmother, was quite noisy. Jeremy's mother was usually drunk and his stepfather, Johnny Moore was a stockbroker. He also drank and had a scarlet face. He was master of the Chiddingfold and Leconfield Hunt. My father found them all rather tiresome and was amazed at the style and comfort in which we lived.

I had changed my mind about becoming a regular soldier as November came along and I had to make a decision. Public duties were getting monotonous and my finances had deteriorated drastically. I had done just over three years as I had been held back in case the Irish Guards were needed in the context of the invasion of Egypt and the Suez fiasco. I made a decision to leave as soon as I could, which I was able to do after Christmas

THE WIDE WORLD

*H*aving left the army, I told my father I thought business
was where I should go. He suggested and arranged for me
to go and work for the Harrison Line. He felt the experience of
knowing how goods were shipped around the world was excellent
training for any branch of commerce or finance. It was indeed as I had
to learn about bills of lading, the difference between CIF and FOB and
geography as well as procuring everything needed for a ship to work.

The offices were in Mincing Lane and I started there mid-
January. I continued to live at Wellington Court but no longer
enjoyed the services of Guardsman Wood. Wearing a suit, stiff collar,
bowler hat and rolled umbrella, I left at about 8.15 am, walked to
Knightsbridge Tube station and got the Tube to Bank with a change
at Holborn. I walked from Bank to the office for a 9 am start. I was
paid about £25 per month and got luncheon vouchers worth 3
shillings and sixpence, which was sufficient to buy an adequate meal
in a huge basement restaurant under Plantation House, just opposite
the offices.

The Harrison Line had about twenty-five ships and ran a freight
service form the West Indies and Gulf to Liverpool and London.
There was also a similar service from South Africa and all up the East

Coast of Africa and a service from India, Pakistan, and Ceylon. Containers were unheard of and commodities were shipped in sacks.

My first job was in the inward-freight department, which involved dealing with all the documentation for goods arriving in London and their onward dispatch to wherever. The outward-freight department dealt with the dispatch of what was taken to the docks for export. There was an enormous paper trail, which involved a lot of filing so every item could be traced if there was a problem such as damage in transit or a consignment going missing.

I spent a week doing this very boring job but it was usually done by a young girl – the proverbial filing clerk.

One week, there was a terrific rumpus as a mass of documentation could not be found. A particularly bolshie girl had been doing the filing and then just did not turn up for work anymore. A bulging file, labelled Miscellaneous, was duly found and this girl had just dumped everything into it. After four months I had a slight promotion and went to work for Mr Brockman. He was a rather prickly character who was responsible for provisioning all our ships when they were in London, paying the crews, refuelling and most things, excepting the cargos. On the arrival of a ship, we'd go to the relevant dock, which was usually the West India Docks, in Mr Brockman's car, and we'd park alongside. To get into the docks, he had a pass that had to be shown to the police.

At the quay, we would go on board where we'd conduct a pay parade, which was paid out in cash that we had brought with us. We'd be handed a huge list of provisions required, together with requests for rope, paint, and things for maintaining the ship. On departure, we would be stopped at the gate where Brockman would hand the policeman his pass that had a 10-shilling note in it. The policeman would pocket it and we'd be on our way. On arrival back at the office, there would be a case of Scotch, which had not been there when we'd left the office. If he was in a good mood, he'd sometimes give me a bottle of duty-free Scotch. I'd then have to settle down and order the paint, rope, etc.

Liverpool was the head office but we had two directors in London. All the ships were named after occupations, like Planter, Forester, etc.

The company was privately owned by the Harrison family and Sir Thomas Pilkington whose mother was a Harrison. In May, the London office moved to Fountain House, one of the first high-rise office blocks, which surprisingly is still there today, just off Fenchurch Street.

Social life continued much as before with cocktail parties and dances when the summer started. We continued to entertain in Wellington Court. Then Michael Boyle told me he had been given his father's 12-metre yacht and would I like to come and be a crew at weekends in Cowes. This was one of the largest yachts sailing in the UK at this time.

We had a lot of fun with large parties of boys and girls, sailing by day and sleeping on board by night. I could not sail every weekend as I was in the office until lunchtime on alternate Saturdays.

We had a great time during Cowes week at the end of which we were competing in the Fastnet Race. We had a crew of twelve, which included Penelope Morogh-Bernard and Sara Curtis who were cooking. We had Colin Ratsey from the sailmakers of that name, Duncan sometimes known as drunken, Hamilton the famous racing driver who brought along Jumbo Goddard who was a sort of professional yachtsman. He had been Bosun on the replica of the Mayflower, which had sailed to Jamestown from England the previous year. We also had the manager of the Midland Bank in Cowes who was a very experienced sailor, always known as Banky Bill.

There was also Albert Pengelly, Michael's skipper who had been the topsail man as a boy in Britannia in the twenties. He spent the entire race in Britannia at the cross-trees up the mast and he could not swim.

For the Fastnet, we were the scratch boat. We started in the morning in a Force-9 gale from the West with as many reefs as possible in the mainsail. We tacked down the Solent and by Yarmouth, we had lost our Genoa, which just disintegrated. By the Needles, we had lost more sails. At about this stage, everyone was wet, cold, and hungry so it was agreed the girls could not cook but they would produce marmalade sandwiches. I helped them open a 12 lb tin and we all duly ate our fill. We then replaced the tin in a locker that was up under the deck midships, adjacent to the galley. Sometime later, we hit a particularly large wave. The locker flew open and about 10lb of marmalade landed on the floor.

By the time we got to Portland, we had no sails left. The main had torn, all headsails had gone, and then the storm jib tore at the cleat. It was decided to retire from the race and start the engine. It would not start and my memories are of Duncan Hamilton on the floor by the engine with it in bits, his friend Jumbo Goddard on the foredeck in shorts trying to mend the storm jib, and me and the girls trying to clear up the marmalade. There was no engine, and no sails so Banky Bill took over and said we must sail under bare poles back to Portsmouth round the Isle of Wight.

This is what we did and arrived there in the small hours of the next morning. Of course, with hindsight, we were totally unprepared with rotten, old cotton sails. That was the end of sailing for the summer but Sara Curtis then started to come into my life.

Living in Wellington Court with Michael Boyle and Jeremy Durham Matthews had many advantages as they were still serving soldiers and I had the benefit of their soldier servants.

At this time, Ethel Beddington also came into my life. She was the sister of my father's elder brother's wife. She was a widow who lived in a huge flat in Grosvenor Square. She was a great party-giver who collected people. She was also very eccentric in as much all the furniture was covered in plastic, as were the bricks that acted as door stoppers. She had her coffin under her bed.

There were all sorts of people at her parties to which I always got an invitation. One evening, I was smothered in a hug by Sophie Tucker. Her husband Claude Beddington was a rich stockbroker who had been born Nathaniel Moses but changed his name. When this was gazetted in the London Gazette and he went on to the floor of the stock exchange, someone pinned a piece of paper on his back which read, 'And the Lord said unto Moses, in the morning I will call you Beddington'.

As the summer had gone on, I was becoming increasingly fed up with the job. I was working with nice people but travel on the Tube and life, in general, was not yet for me. In late July, I met up with my brother Nick at a drinks party. He had just finished with the army after his two years of national service.

Neither of us had found any girl we wanted to take to dinner and so we went to the Guards Club for some dinner. My brother explained that he had always had a plan after the army to go to Australia with Tony Rowcliffe who had been at Cheam and Eton with him. Tony failed his army medical so for the past two years, he had been working and studying to become a land agent/surveyor. He knew his father would cut him off if he gave up and he had hopes of inheriting the family estate in Wiltshire. My brother said it was very disappointing and he was wondering whether it would be the same on his own. I had not given it any real thought but I said I hated the job I was doing and I would go with him.

When we told our parents of our plans, they were very philosophical but we hardly knew what a shock it really was to them. We promised to write regularly. Father bought us tickets on the Orontes sailing mid-September with a two-birth cabin, and I resigned from the Harrison Line who wished me good luck but said I was giving up what could have been a very promising career in shipping.

AUSTRALIA

ather and Mother drove us to Tilbury and saw us off on Orontes, an old P&O liner with just one class of passenger. The passengers were a mixed bunch. Many were travelling to Australia for £10 to emigrate there. They would have to work for a number of years as ordered by the Australian Government. There were lots of Australian girls returning home from doing Europe while Australian men were doing national service and then there were business people returning and others who were going to visit family. Our cabin was small but had a porthole and was certainly one of the better one.

For meals, everyone was placed at a table. We were with the first officer and about eight others. I only remember one man who I asked what he did for a living. He replied he was a salesman. I asked what he sold and his reply was that the article was immaterial.

Everything was a bit basic. There was no swimming pool and the only real exercise was deck tennis, which was like volleyball but played with a rubber ring. I was never a good Fives player but I found I was good at this game.

When we got to the Mediterranean, the weather became sunny and warm. My skin was not unused to the sun, having spent nearly two years in Egypt but my brother had little experience of it. While on deck, he wore a white nylon non-iron shirt. Sadly, this was no protector from the sun and my poor brother came out with awful sunburn on his back and shoulders with blisters. It took some time to heel up but he has never really sunbathed again.

We both made friends of some of the Australian girls and life was fun.

It took twenty-eight days to get to Fremantle in West Australia. On the way, we stopped in Gibraltar to get fresh provisions. We then stopped at Port Said, which brought back memories, and Aden where we were able to go ashore and have a look around. Our final stop was Colombo, where we stayed for twenty-four hours, which enabled us to get a taxi with two others and have a good look around the island. One memory was of a huge Tamil wedding in a village with a river through it on which were a large number of exotically decorated floats. It was exceptionally colourful.

By the time we got to Freemantle, life was getting a bit complicated and my brother had two girls rather fighting over him. We decided to get off Orontes there rather than go on and try our luck in Western Australia. We took a train up to Perth along the Swan River and found ourselves a hotel at the west end of St George's Terrace. It had a large car park in front of it. We soon found out about Australia's attitude to alcohol. In Perth, bars closed at 6 pm but you could get a drink with a meal in a hotel provided the hotel had a licence, which ours did not.

We got a room overlooking this car park and were unpacking our things. We had a large number of letters of introduction to people all over Australia. These had been provided by father, friends of his, and anyone we knew who had a friend or relation in Australia.

I was sorting these out to see what we had for Western Australia when we saw a large bus come into the car park. Out of it got the band of the Irish Guards who were on a world tour. In charge was John Head who had been briefly senior subaltern when I joined the battalion in Egypt. There was also Captain Jigs Jaeger, the famous director of music of the Irish Guards and a good friend. We went down to greet them. Jigs and John were staying at Government House. The band were in our hotel. They were giving a concert the following night in the City Hall.

We carried on with our unpacking and then went for a walk to discover Perth. We called at Government House and signed our names in the book in the lodge.

To our surprise, we were telephoned the following day at our hotel by David Stuart Menzies, who had been a contemporary at Eton. He was ADC to the governor who was Lt General Sir Charles Gardiner. He asked whether we had dinner jackets with us and was rather surprised when we said we did at our father's suggestion. We were promptly invited to dinner at Government House the following night. In our dinner jackets and black tie, we arrived promptly at 7 pm. It turned out that Eve Gardiner, his wife, had known and was an admirer of our father in Ireland when he had parted from his first wife in the 1920s. Sir Charles only had one leg but had been a very fine polo player. After dinner, he instructed David, his ADC, to bring him his knitting and this very distinguished retired general sat there talking and knitting. Needless to say, John Head and Jigs were at dinner as were another two couples who were fascinated by what we thought we were going to do.

The next day, we started calling up those people in Western Australia to whom we had letters of introduction. We both wanted to go up to the north and get jobs on a big station with sheep and cattle. The first offer came from Aubrey Hardie who had two stations up near Port Hedland, one inland run by his son John and one on the coast run by his nephew Peter. He was a gruff and slightly grim old man with no ostensible sense of humour. He said he would employ us from early January but he would expect us to stay for a year. We would not get any favours or fancy accommodation and would be paid as station hands the minimum wage. This was very good as most young people coming to Australia looking for jobs like us were classed as jackaroos, lived in the house or homestead with the family, and paid a pittance.

Next, an offer came from Sir Ernest Lee Steere via a letter of introduction from Patience his sister-in-law who lived at Jayes Park in

Ockley near home. He said he would gladly give us work on his farm at Toodjay about 100 miles from Perth. He went further and said he would be driving up there the following afternoon and would take us with him.

His wife Jackie was a good looking but notoriously tough woman. She was hard-drinking and hard-swearing and suggested we might not be up to physical farm work. On the drive to Toodjay, we stopped twice for refreshments. Jackie was clearly intent on getting us drunk and the drinks came fast and furious. I don't think she realised she was dealing with two ex-Irish Guards officers and much to Ernest's amusement, the only person drunk when we arrived was Jackie.

It was about 5000 acres of mixed farming, cattle, sheep, and arable land, with a lovely Irish man, Joe Broderick, in charge. He was originally from Dublin and very knowledgeable about horses. We were billeted in a room used by shearers when they visited, and we ate most of our meals with the Broderick family. They had many horses and we started riding quite a lot. Joe was very helpful in preparing us for what to expect when we went north. We also had to learn how to kill and cut up a sheep. Under instruction from Joe, we each killed our first sheep by cutting its throat, then skinning it, which requires a technique that you need to learn. You then saw it in half down the spine, having removed the head. Each half gives you basically a leg, a shoulder and lots of chops and cutlets. It was a new experience but we had been brought up on a farm at home. In the north and here, the main diet of all who worked on a farm or station was lamb or mutton. There always seemed to be plenty of work to do. We repaired fences and handled sheep and cattle. We spent a jolly Christmas with the Lee Steere family.

Then it was goodbye and back to Perth and Freemantle to board a ship to Port Hedland. We stopped at Government House and left our dinner jackets there for safekeeping. The first port of call was Carnavon and then Port Hedland where we were met by John and Peter Hardie in the Esplanade Hotel. My brother elected to go to

Peter Hardie at Boodarie, which was on the coast about 25 miles south of Port Hedland and perhaps a bit less hot than Warralong Station, which was run by John Hardie. It was inland about 100 miles east on the road to Marble Bara, a small mining town, and the hottest place in Australia. We then went to the Elder Smiths store where we topped up on some clothing; khaki cotton shirts and shorts and green army surplus cotton trousers for riding in addition to a pair of high-heeled boots, again for riding. I said goodbye to my brother. Then in a Holden ute (utility), which is a car cab with an open truck back, we set off inland on dirt roads, putting up a huge trail of dust. The temperature was well over 100 degrees but no humidity.

After about 80 miles, we turned off the main road onto a rougher station road. Here was what was called the outstation, which was manned by a half-Aborigine and his wife who were employees of Warralong. Also, there was a range of large buildings where the sheep were sheared once a year. We drove for a further 25 miles or so until we arrived at the station homestead itself.

Warralong was over 750,000 acres of spinifex grass and scrub with belts of gum trees situated in dried-up river beds. The land around the homestead was fenced into more-or-less 20,000-acre paddocks and about 40,000 sheep were kept. These were merinos and kept for their wool. Over a third of the land was taken up by that part south of Port Hedland to Marble Bar Road, which was largely unfenced but where some 2000 cattle wandered more-or-less wild.

The homestead itself was a small single-storey house built of wood and tin with a veranda all around. John Hardie lived there. A bit away was another wood-and-tin building with three rooms and a simple shower room and loo. John Fisher who was John's No 2, lived in one of the rooms there. I was in the middle room and Terry Smith was in the other. John was a year younger than me but had worked at Warralong since leaving school at seventeen. He was intelligent and from a good family, and we became good friends. Smith was perfectly nice but not very bright.

There was then another building with housing accommodation for the cook and his wife. There was also the kitchen and area where we all ate together. Everywhere you sit, eat or sleep in the outback of

Australia has to be fly proof because the further you are away from anything, the worse are the flies.

There were a number of other buildings, mostly made of tin, which acted as stores. This included a large workshop building that was John Hardie's domain. It was fully equipped and John was an excellent mechanic who could repair anything and even made spare parts on a lathe. If a vehicle broke down, you repaired it as there were no mechanics that side of Port Hedland. There was a mail lorry that came by once a week between Port Hedland and Marble Bar. It brought the mail and could bring spare parts and provisions from Port Hedland or further away.

Finally, there was a small encampment of huts that housed three Aborigines who were available to help with moving sheep or cattle when required. Under the Australian system of the time, they were not full citizens and so not entitled to the minimum wage that we enjoyed. Under that system, they could apply for citizenship but had to prove a level of education, literacy, and understanding that was usually out of their reach. They were good with horses but very bad with vehicles or any heavy work like driving in fence posts or digging holes. They were also unreliable as they would go off on holiday or walkabout as they called it, without giving any notice.

After a meal of lamb/mutton and potatoes, we'd all turn in for the night.

Breakfast was at 6.30 am, after which I would be taken out and allocated four horses together with a wonderful large comfortable stock saddle and other tack. This would be mine to look after. You rotated the use of each of your four horses and the ones you were not currently riding were set loose in a paddock of about 500 acres with hobbles on their front feet. Any work to do with moving sheep anywhere and also the cattle had to be done on horseback as spinifex grass is in clumps and no way could you ride a motor bicycle or drive a vehicle across it.

Windmills were the source of water and were positioned at the corners of the fenced 20,000-acre blocks and connected by station roads which had to be maintained. The windmills pumped water up from the plentiful amounts underground into tanks that supplied troughs out of which the sheep drank. A malfunctioning windmill and an empty tank would lead to the early deaths of sheep in that great heat so a daily task for one person was to drive around and inspect the windmills to see that they were operational where the sheep were.

There were vastly more kangaroos than sheep on the land and they competed for the grazing. There was an effort made to control their numbers by shooting. There was a collection of .45 Winchester rifles as used by John Wayne in the movies, which we used to shoot kangaroos as we did the windmill rounds. I am afraid we just left the carcases there but they soon disappeared, eaten by ants and termites.

If we had pigs at the homestead, we used to feed them on kangaroo. It produced a very fierce pig and very strong-flavoured pork. The stocking rate for sheep was about one sheep to 40 acres and so 5,000 sheep would eat out a 20,000 block of land in a number of weeks. Thus, moving mobs of sheep onto fresh pasture using horses was a regular job that required at least four or five horsemen. For probably three days a week, we would all be out moving sheep, two days doing windmill runs and repairing fences, and one day in the workshop.

There were wild horses and camels too. The latter had been let loose when lorries replaced camel trains moving the wool, and they were a menace as a camel caught in a fence could pull up half a mile of fencing. All the fences were metal posts and plain wire. Wooden posts would have been eaten rapidly by white ants.

We ate a lot of lamb/mutton, breakfast chops and eggs. Lunch was cold and dinner roasted. Thus, John, Terry, or I had to kill twice a week. This involved saddling a horse and going to a 200-acre paddock where we had put a number of wethers, fatter castrated sheep. You selected a likely looking one, jumped off your horse, scragged it, lifted it onto the saddle, climbed back on board and rode back. There you would kill the sheep, skin it, and then take it to the cookhouse where the cook butchered it. He had, in fact, worked in a butcher's shop in England before getting with his wife a £10 assisted passage to Australia and finishing up working at Warralong.

Twice during the year that I was there, we spent a week dealing with the cattle. We'd camp out most of those nights to get an early start. There were two sets of cattle yards into one of which we'd drive about 100 head of cattle at a time. We'd then draft out the cows and calves. We'd apply a hot brand to unbranded animals and castrate young bulls. Previously castrated bullocks were separated out to be sold. It was exhausting work but at the end of the week, we'd have about 300 young bullocks for sale. It was pretty crude cattle ranching but I understand the return was quite good when they were sold. We'd also acquire a nice young bullock to eat, which was a very welcome change from mutton.

Deep freezers were not really in common use in 1959. Our refrigerators were powered by bottled gas while the generator was for electric light. There was no television and the water was heated by the sun. We drank vast amounts of tea brewed in a billy-can (a 2-litre oil can with no top and a wire handle) with sugar and a bit of powdered milk if we wanted. We had a few, mainly root vegetables but not much fruit or green vegetables.

After about six months, I started to get some sores on my hands and arms, which would not heal. I borrowed a vehicle and drove to Marble Bar where there was a doctor. I found him in the pub a bit the worse for wear. We went back to his house, he looked at my arms and said I was suffering from a lack of fruit, vegetables and Vitamin C. I needed a course of penicillin injections to clear it up. He had dreadful shakes and said it would be much better if I inject myself, and showed me where to put the needle in on my arm. I did so with no problem. He then gave me a syringe and a bottle of penicillin, said keep it all clean with boiling water, and inject myself daily for a week until it was all gone. He also gave me some Vitamin C pills. We had a good laugh when I got back to the station but John said he would put in an order for oranges to come out on the mail truck each week. I must say the sores healed up and I never had a problem again.

All this time, I was earning quite good money with nothing to spend it on except a quart bottle of Swan lager. I'd have that most nights when it got dark and we'd sit and talk before supper on John's veranda. I'd also spend it on tins of rolling tobacco and Rizla cigarette papers. We all smoked but the dry heat caused ordinary cigarettes to dry out so they just burned up. We kept a piece of potato in the tin with the tobacco to keep it moist. I got to the stage where I could roll a cigarette while riding on a horse. The smoke also kept the flies away a bit.

There were lots of snakes, and all very poisonous. If we saw a snake while out in the bush it was an unwritten law that you dismounted from your horse or got out of your vehicle and killed the snake. One of the Aborigines had a mongrel dog that used to kill snakes. As the snake would strike, the dog would withdraw. After this would go on for some time, the snake would get tired and the dog would grab it around the neck.

On one occasion, I was just about to get out of bed and put my foot on the ground when I saw a death adder curled up there. I got the snake killer and, like a good boy, killed it. The snake killer was about six 4-foot lengths of fencing wire twisted together and was very effective.

As far as the sheep were concerned, we took much more care. We had comprehensive yards at strategic intervals on the property for handling sheep. The rams were kept separate and only put in with the ewes some five or six months before lambing. They were then drafted out when the lambs were castrated, which was done with a knife because rubber rings had been found to attract flystrike.

We also performed on young ewes a gruesome operation called mulesing, now illegal I believe. We cut off a slice of skin on either side of the sheep's backside. Like with castration this healed very quickly and resulted in sheep treated in this way not getting struck by flies. If sheep were struck by flies, we dealt with it with shears and disinfectant. By and large, the sheep were very well looked after.

These were sheep for their wool and a major time each year was shearing, which was done in July some six months after we had arrived. All the sheep were moved to be near the shearing shed at the outstation and over about fourteen days, every sheep was sheared by a team of contract shearers. There were about twelve of them and they would each shear between 100 and 200 sheep in a day. The fleeces were graded and packed and compressed into large bales by members of the team.

We just had to keep a constant flow of sheep into the yards and disperse out the shaven sheep. The shearing gangs were about as rough as they come. It was very highly paid back-breaking work in extreme heat and a majority were very crippled by the time they were forty.

After shearing, there was the big social event of the year, the picnic races in Port Hedland. This was a week-long party with races on for about three days. Everyone entered a horse into some sort of race. I had one charming piebald horse called Ranger against whose front legs I could lean out of the sun when we were resting out chasing sheep and cattle. He was reputed to be a half quarter horse as he was very fast off the mark. He also had an extraordinarily hard mouth. I put us in for two sprint races over about four furlongs. There were about twelve horses in the race and we were second in one of them.

One of our recreations was trying to shoot wild pigs in the dry river beds. These were domestic pigs gone wild and there were quite a few of them. We rode out on horses with our Winchester .45 rifles. When we saw a pig, we had to turn the horse to the side and shoot. These rifles were not particularly accurate as we used to load the bullets ourselves. You also had to turn the horse as I found out one day when I fired over the horse's ears and moments later hit the ground having been bucked off.

John Hardie was very much a loner so there was only a little partying on some weekends. This was an opportunity to consume large amounts of Swan lager. There was little wine and those who drank spirits were deemed drunks or winos. However, we did meet a number of owners of neighbouring stations and they seemed to live similar lives. The business of running a station in the Pilbara was fairly marginal and largely depended on the price of wool. Of course, this was before the discovery of the Pilbara iron ore deposits at the south end of Warralong in what we called the Black Hills. This proved to be the biggest iron ore deposit in the world and transformed this whole area some six years later.

I found that when I was not working, I read a lot as John Hardie had a large library in the homestead. I read all that Neville Shute ever wrote and a great amount of history and biography. In many ways, I educated myself. Letters arrived and were sent each week. My mother wrote every week with all news from home and Sara Curtis wrote at least every two weeks with news of friends. Dawn Kettlewell also wrote from time to time with lots of dirty jokes and pornographic poetry.

After being there for nearly a year in November, I arranged to meet up with my brother and go south to Perth. There, we pooled our money and used some of it to buy a new long-wheelbase diesel Land Rover. We called on Aubrey Hardie who seemed to indicate we had been good workers. We then had dinner at Government House and stayed the night there. We took the road to Toodjay to see Lee Steeres and then went back to Port Hedland.

We called at Roeburn where there was the Wittenoom Gorge Blue Asbestos mine where we had been told the wages were very good. We were given a tour but it was very dusty and unpleasant and so we quickly decided it was not for us. This was, of course, the mine that produced the most lethal of all asbestos, blue asbestos. We were given masks and so I just hope none of it got into our lungs. That was a very lucky escape.

I took the Land Rover back to Warralong as we had a better work-shop and my brother had marginally more access to civilisation being quite close to Port Hedland. The first job was to weld up some strong pipe and make a large grill on the front of the Land Rover. This acted as protection against kangaroos jumping in front of you. We also hung two waterbags from hooks in front so we always had cold water to drink and you did drink a lot in that heat.

I bought and John Hardie helped me install a copper tank that took about 10 gallons of water. We also installed and fixed a 45-gallon drum for diesel so we could do long distances.

We met up with Peter Hardie, my brother, and his team at Boodarie for Christmas day and then drove our Land Rover North to Broome. We had our swags with us. These consisted of an oversize waterproof ground sheet, a thin mattress, a sheet, a pillow, a blanket, and a sleeping bag. By day, they were rolled up and secured with a large leather strap. By night they were unrolled and were very good beds in all temperatures. Later on, we could even continue sleeping with rain or a heavy dew by wrapping the sides of the groundsheet over ourselves. We spent two nights on a 100-mile beach effectively camping. It was totally deserted. We did not swim due to fear of sharks but we found rock oysters, which we prised off the rocks and cooked in the embers of a fire. We visited Broome and then went towards the Kimberley but felt we ought to get back and so never made it to Go Go the Emmanuel Station, to which we had an invitation.

Back at Warralong soon afterwards, we suddenly had rain in the night and then all day. There was about 14 inches of it. The dry river beds became raging torrents 500-yards wide and we were completely cut off for days. The desert then bloomed with flowers everywhere and that was the rain for another year.

By the middle of January, it was time to move on. We said our goodbyes and went to Perth, said goodbye there to the Gardiners, Aubrey Hardie, and Lee Steeres. Before leaving, we had a metal cage fabricated in Perth, which went underneath the fabric canopy over the rear of our Land Rover. It had a metal gate that could be locked with a padlock. We drove to Kalgoorlie where there was a bit of gold mining still in operation and then set off across the Nullarbor plain to Adelaide, some 1200 miles of nothing.

My brother had loved working with horses, in particular, and I had fallen in love with the country and the life, despite the total lack of female company. It was a hard life but a good one. We both reckoned it was a wonderful experience.

ROUND AUSTRALIA

$\mathcal{H}$aving left Perth, we took the road to Kalgoorlie, which was a real dump in the desert. The price of gold was not good and gold mining was in the doldrums there. We camped for the night.

We now had a fold-up canvas bed each with our swags. On the side of the vehicle, we had a tent that rolled up into two brackets while moving and which let down with an aluminium frame to the ground, open to the rear. This gave us a sheltered area where we had our two beds, a folding table, and two folding chairs. Through a tap in the side of the vehicle, we could access fresh water from our tank or from the waterbags on the front.

We cooked over a fire which we could always find wood for. When we could not get fresh food or meat, our favourite meal was tins of stewed steak and whatever else we had. It took very little time to let down and erect our tent. Our beds, swags, table and chairs and our luggage all went in the back with the water tank and 45-gallon drum for diesel together with tools. It was quite a payload and so apart from not being very comfortable, our top speed was about 65 mph.

We then set off across the Nullarbor plain, 1200 miles of desert and scrub with nothing else.

On arrival in Adelaide, we looked up Mrs Ayres to whom Ethel Beddington, a very eccentric sort of aunt, had written. She was the elderly sister of the legendary Sid Kidman who was a pioneer of opening up the outback. The family had big properties in the Northern Territory. Her niece was Anne Kidman who was our age. She, with her friend Margy Hone, set out to show us Adelaide and give us a good time. About the second night, we went to a nightclub with a gang of her friends. We ordered drinks, for a change and not just beer. About half an hour later, the staff appeared and removed all the glasses with our drinks. It was 9 pm. About 10 minutes later, they came back with many small teapots and cups. It was not tea but all our drinks back. The law was that no alcohol was to be sold after 9 pm but if the police had called, they would see we were only drinking tea and coffee.

We also had a letter to Sir Tom Barr Smith to whom we had written ahead. He invited us to dinner in our dinner jackets. He was a big businessman as chairman of the stock agents, Elder Smith, and one of the richest men in Australia. He lived in great style in a house in Adelaide, which was surrounded by a high fence and wall. We drove up in our dirty Land Rover to be greeted by two footmen in sort of livery. It was a large party. We reminded him that he owned the largest and probably best property outside Port Hedland. 'Yes,' he said but he could not remember its name! He started to find great interest in what we had been doing and our plans.

We decided to move on and after provisioning, we set off north for Alice Springs. We stopped at the Coober Pedy opal-mining area. This consisted of a mass of small mines being dug out by hand by single individuals in rocky, desolate ground. We camped on the way to Alice Springs and travel was all on red dirt roads for miles upon miles, and nothing but kangaroos and the odd emu.

After Alice Springs, which was a very small town, we went on to Ayers Rock, which was a huge red rock in the middle of nowhere. Allegedly, originally a comet from outer space, and now, a huge tourist attraction and a very precious place to the Aborigines. There was nothing there; not even an Aborigine. We wandered around the place and climbed a bit but there was nothing else to see.

Our plan was to go on to Darwin on the north coast but it suddenly rained very hard, which made us decide to change our plan. Our destination then was Sydney. Anyhow, we turned right and east towards Cloncurry and Mount Isa. It was a difficult trip. We rescued a woman in a Holden ute who was stuck in a river that was rising, by pulling her out backwards. We then had to wait until the river went down sufficiently to get across it.

Nick and I had a row as to whether it was low enough or not but I prevailed and drove across safely. Nick then had to wade through the river, which did not improve his humour. We then came to a larger river and had to cross on a disused railway bridge, keeping two wheels on one of the rails. Nick walked in front and guided me while I drove.

The rain stopped and we got to Cloncurry and Mount Isa. The latter was miles from anywhere and had a predominantly male population. The consumption of beer was fourteen pints per person per day of the population as it was very hot. We discovered we had no real connections in Sydney and so we missed Brisbane and Sydney and drove to Canberra. There, my good friend Billy Stanier of the Welsh Guards was ADC to Field Marshall Sir Bill Slim, the Governor-General of Australia. Billy showed us Canberra, which was the new federal capital being carved out of the bush. It was all building works everywhere. We met the field marshal who was a wonderful craggy old man.

We then went on to call on Ken and Lydia Crawford who were farming at Albany on the NSW/Victoria border. They had a lovely farm and were grateful for a bit of help with drenching and dipping their sheep. Lydia was very elegant and from the Reynella wine family in South Australia. Ken had been in the Gordon Highlanders during the war, after which he returned to farming. He changed for dinner each night into a black tie and a white mess jacket so our dinner jackets came in useful once again.

We had people to look up in Melbourne and so we drove down there. Ken Crawford had insisted we stayed in the Melbourne Club as his guests in return for all the work we had done on his farm. This was large, old fashioned and not very busy. The staff were mainly ex-British army with a splendid Life Guard sergeant major who woke us in the morning in our room with a gentle shake before telling us the weather and asking what we would like for breakfast.

On our second night there, we got talking with an old member who was fascinated by where we had come from. He told us he had a society meeting the following evening (I can't remember whether it was geographical or something else). Anyhow, in exchange for dinner, we gave a talk to about thirty older Australians. I talked about the country and way of life and Nick talked about sheep and what we did with them. It was a great success as it seemed none of them had ever really been out of the city.

We also had a letter of introduction to Sir Norman Martin who was the British Agent-General in Victoria.

We telephoned him and he seemed somewhat nonplussed as to what he could do with us. On an off chance he said did we play golf. We said, 'Yes,' and so he said he would get a partner and we should come and meet at the Royal Melbourne Golf Club and we would have a game. We duly arrived and Sir Norman turned out to be about sixty and rather serious. He had brought his friend Sir Edward Myers who was chairman of the family's largest retailer in Australia. We played a four-ball, us against them.

Being a bit mean, I suggested my brother teed off first. He hit his ball about thirty yards into a bush. I did not do much better and after nine holes we were seven down and our opponents were wondering why they had agreed to play with such obviously hopeless young men. Anyhow, we suddenly came good and won the match on the seventeenth green two up. I think they thought we were having them on but the reality was we had not played for 18 months.

Time was moving on and we booked a passage for ourselves to Durban in South Africa. We'd go on the Southern Cross from Melbourne in about three weeks' time and book passage for our Land Rover on a cargo ship. We thought we must see Sydney so we stayed a night with the Crawfords and went with them to their house in Palm Beach, north of Sydney. It was lovely and I had the first swim in the sea since Perth. After a few days, we went and saw the Opera House, which was under construction, and looked around Sydney.

While with the Crawfords, we got a telegram from our mother asking us to telephone. This involved going to a post office and booking a call at a cost of £1 per minute. We did this at about 11.30 am and were told to come back at 3 pm as the call was booked for that time. When we got back there was a further delay of thirty minutes and then the call came through and we heard our mothers voice for the first time in eighteen months. Her call was to say Father had been very ill and in Guy's Hospital but worry was over and he was now better. She did not want us to cut short our trip. We had, of course, told her what we had done and proposed to do in great detail in our letters.

We then drove back to Melbourne. There, we stayed with some lovely people in one of the smart suburbs before going to the docks, giving our Land Rover to the shipping agents, and getting on the Sothern Cross.

AFRICA, HERE WE COME

The Southern Cross sailed from Melbourne with some very nice people on board who were returning to Africa or home to England. We got to know Tim Mason and his wife, who were returning to Port Elisabeth, and the Symons to Abercorn on Lake Tanganyika where he was the district commissioner.

We had a cheap cabin, sharing with four others, and so spent as little time in it as possible. It was a more modern ship than Orontes with more deck facilities. We stopped at Adelaide and then Freemantle but then went onto Durban. A major activity was deck tennis, which I had played on our way out to Australia. I played with the ship's officers and also a knock-out competition for the passengers, in the final where I beat a fifty-year-old Australian barrister who had played Davis-Cup tennis. I had suddenly found a quite useless activity at which I was very good as I could beat all the ship's officers who played all the time.

On arrival in Durban, we had invited ourselves to stay with Malcolm Thompson and his wife Elisabeth. He was the Harrison Line representative in Durban and we had been in the London office together. They had a large house rented from the Rennie family in Kloof with a big garden and a huge avocado pear tree. They were newly married and newly arrived so we spent over two weeks with them waiting for our Land Rover to arrive on its cargo ship.

My lack of female company over the past year or more was suddenly rectified when Sara Curtis arrived in Durban from her sister in Kenya. It was wonderful to see her and, probably rather reluctantly, my brother agreed she could accompany us on our travels.

Malcolm introduced us to friends of theirs, the Kimbers, who had a lovely farm near Pietermaritzburg and the now-three of us spent a long weekend up there, exploring the area around the Howick Falls.

On one day we got up early and drove up to the Orange Free State and a farm to shoot guinea fowl. There was a square plantation of about ten acres of gum trees with a wide ride at each side of the square. We stood in the ride and about 100 beaters rounded up lots of guinea fowl grazing in the fields around and drove them over the wood where we shot at them. After the drive had finished, we walked through the wood to the other side by which time the beaters had run round the guinea fowl grazing the other side, and they then drove them back over the plantation. This manoeuvre was carried out a number of times.

By now it was May 1959 and so we left in the Land Rover with Sara in the middle seat. Our first night was on a lovely beach near New London where we camped with all the facilities we had last used in Australia. We had got a swag for Sara and another camp bed. We got some wood, lit a fire, and cooked dinner and I had a swim in the morning. We drank coffee and then went on to Port Elisabeth. We went across the desolate Transkei, which was barren and grazed out, to Port Elisabeth where we had dinner with the Masons from the Southern Cross. They advised us to stay in a hotel, which was a change from camping.

Then, we went on down to Cape Town where we had a letter of introduction to Ken Fisher. He was the Coast Lines representative in South Africa. We told him we intended to drive our Land Rover home all the way up Africa. He introduced us to Mitchell Cotts who were forwarding agents and agents for all sorts of companies. They had offices in every big town or city in nearly all of Africa so we were sort of passed from one Mitchell Cotts office to another. We sorted out visas in Cape Town as we would require them for many countries on our way. Apartheid had not yet led every country to break off with South Africa and so pretty nearly every country in Africa had a consulate or Embassy in Cape Town. Our passports were filled up with visas.

We did all the usual sights like Table Mountain and were lucky enough to be able to stay in Fisher's guest house. We also purchased a .275 rifle and a Smith and Wesson six-shot revolver as we planned to shoot for the pot in suitable places. We also acquired a large icebox, which would take big blocks of ice. The ice blocks were surprisingly quite easy to buy in many places. This would allow us to keep food and fruit and some vegetables but we also bought a stock of tins.

We then set off to go north to south-west Africa and the Etosha Pan area. Camping on the way, we shot a springbok near the Orange River. We skinned and cooked it over a fire. We kept the balance of the meat in our cool box, which made for a number of meals.

We went on to Windhoek and then further north where we stopped in a very small town at a general store to get some provisions and ice. Here we got into conversation with a very friendly local farmer who after a bit of time asked us whether we had a rifle. We wondered what his interest was but he seemed a good man and so we admitted we did. He promptly invited us to come out to his farm and do some shooting. That sounded fun and so we followed him out into the bush and a rather humble farm.

We spent two days shooting buck including a large kudu. He was very hospitable and we realised that what we were doing was filling his larder with biltong as he cut up everything we shot and put it out in the sun to dry.

We then went on to the Etosha where there was a primitive camp and a number of rangers and game wardens. They were hunting a rogue lion and so they asked us whether we would like to shoot a lion. We declined but went with them out into the bush at night where a large bit of meat was hung on a post. The pride of lions arrived and took it but the one they wanted to shoot was not there.

We saw incredible numbers of animals in the area but were not allowed to shoot anything for the pot as it was a national park. There were certainly no tourists. One day, we went fishing in a river where we should have caught tigerfish but we were unlucky.

We decided not to go north into Angola but remembered the Kimbers were having a party near Pietermaritzburg and so we set off across Botswana to Mafeking. We met up with bushmen in the desert. We camped and shot our dinner on the way to a very good party with the Kimbers where we again said goodbye to the Thompsons.

Our next stop was Lourenço Marques in Mozambique, which was run by the Portuguese. This was a thriving and exciting city on the sea without apartheid. Anyone could get the vote if they qualified by education, job, and paying taxes regardless of race. This is where South Africans went for a good time away from the rather rigid laws that, for example, prohibited the pouring of a drink in front of a woman. Of course, with hindsight, very few Africans had the vote but there was an impression of a multicultural society.

We then went over the Zambesi at Beit Bridge and north to the Wankie Game area and then the Victoria Falls. From there, we went to see the Kariba Dam that was being built, which was a gigantic under-taking. It would, when finished, produce an enormous lake and elec-tricity. Then off we went to Bulawayo via the Zimbabwe ruins, which were very interesting. No one seemed to know who had built this town or whatever but the ruins indicated quite a conurbation.

We had been told to call on the Towla Ranch, which was owned by the Liebigs, who made Bovril. It was a huge ranch with a mass of Zebu cattle. We were taken into a huge dining hall where about 120 Africans were eating lunch at trestle tables. I noted that some of the Africans had very black shiny skin and others were grey. I asked whether this indicated different tribes only to be told that the Africans spent eight months working at Towla and four months back on their farms. At Towla, they had a largely meat diet while at the farm, it was mainly maize. The very grey ones had just come back from the farm while the black shiny ones were about to go to their farms. It was all about diet.

When we arrived in Salisbury (Harare) we became aware of a different attitude between white and black; a more liberal one. Sara left us in Salisbury and flew back up to her sister in Kenya where she promised to be when we got there.

We decided to go north by way of Nyasaland (Malawi) and Lake Nyasa. It was all quite fertile land. Then, our route took us through the Luangwa Valley, which was a wonderful game reserve, to Abercorn at the bottom of Lake Tanganyika where we stayed with the Symons who we met on the Southern Cross.

As district commissioner, he had a large motorboat with cabins. He used this for visiting his district, which went all the way up to Kigoma. We joined him for three days on a trip around the area he was responsible for, which was very interesting.

We then drove up the west side of Tanganyika, camping on the way until we got to Rwanda Burundi. It was a very hilly and quite wonderfully beautiful country, which was well populated and farmed. We then went into the Belgian Congo at Bukavu, which was a large town and the centre of the Belgian administration in this area of this huge country.

Just outside the town, we were overtaken by a large American car that waved us down. This turned out to be Bill Turnbull who wanted to know what our number plate MB24 stood for. We told him Marble Bar in Australia. He was Australian and promptly asked us to come and stay at his magnificent house on a hill overlooking Lake Kivu and surrounded by about 1000 acres of coffee.

In the distance on the other side of Kivu were the Ruwenzori mountains with smoke from the odd volcano. Kivu was full of islands and altogether breathtakingly beautiful. Bill came to England in 1961 and we met and had lunch. He told me things were very difficult and dangerous in the Congo. About a year later, it was reported in the papers that Bill and some other farmers had made a last stand at his house against an overwhelming force of marauding Africans and they had all perished.

From Bill, we thought we would then make our way to Stanleyville on the Congo River. This took us through a huge area of forest interlaced with rivers where we needed to cross by various sorts of ferries.

On the way, there was an area called Epulu, which was the home to a large herd of okapi (we were told the only one in Africa) and pygmy elephants as well as proper human pygmies.

At Stanleyville, it was raining and we were advised not to go further west as the roads/tracks were likely to become blocked by flooding. We ascertained that there was a road/track that would take us north to Lake Albert and then into Uganda. On Lake Albert, we met up with some Europeans from Kampala. They invited us to join them fishing for Nile perch. We went out in a boat and hand lined. A gentle nudge and you hauled in your line to find a 40 lb fish on it, which was like a sack of potatoes. The largest caught was about 60 lbs. We ate some fish over a fire for dinner but I have tasted better. By contrast, when we got to the dock the whole village descended on us and took every fish.

Our next stop was at the Murchison Falls where the White Nile is forced through a very narrow gorge. There was a game lodge here, which consisted of a number of Rondavels inside a fence to keep the animals out. It was self-catering and so we camped inside the fence. The following day we took a boat ride down the Nile. There were hundreds of elephants and crocodiles on the banks, which was a fabulous sight.

Then, via Kampala, we arrived in Kenya where we had lots of contacts. First, we went to Molo and found the Pelly farm; she was Sara's sister and so I had a reunion with Sara. They farmed pyrethrum in what were known as the White Highlands. We then made contact with Peter Barclay who had been in the Irish Guards with us. He had taken over from his father a very large farm at Meningai. Old Hugh Barclay was still living there and we had messages for him from my friend and cousin Mungo Park who had worked in Kenya after the war. The Barclays were pioneer settlers.

We spent nearly six weeks in Kenya, went down to the coast near Mombasa, and went to a dinner night with the Coldstream Guards who were stationed at Gilgil. Tom Mboya, a very charismatic Kenya politician who was much feared came to dinner and was absolutely charming and very interesting.

A highlight was Peter Barclay inviting us to go on a trip into the

Northern Frontier Districts and do some shooting. He brought a lorry from the farm and a number of his Africans who pitched tents and catered to all our needs. We shot sand grouse and quite a few buck. Peter wanted to shoot a buffalo that we stalked and shot but he did not totally kill it. We followed in thickish bush with me carrying a reserve rifle and fortunately, when it emerged preparing to charge, Peter finished it off.

We also stayed with Arthur Cole in the Rift Valley at his house and farm. We had a guinea fowl shoot there where they pushed the birds off a high cliff. This was Happy Valley and we were amused that the order of dress for dinner was pyjamas – not too much to take off for friendly relations after dinner.

It was now nearly November and so we set off north to go to Addis Ababa then through the Sudan and Egypt to the Mediterranean. We were counselled to be very careful where we camped in the north of Kenya as there were marauding Shifta tribesman who could be danger- ous. Up till now, we had had no unpleasant experiences with locals. When we got safely to the Ethiopian border, we had a problem. We had to pay a large amount of tax in Ethiopian currency but you couldn't buy that outside Ethiopia and they would not accept Kenyan currency. Anyhow, there was a deal to be done in the black market and we parted with about £100, which we were told we could get back in Addis Ababa as it was a substantial sum out of our funds.

Our first night in Ethiopia was with the British Consul in Southern Ethiopia who lived in a fortified compound with two companies of East African Askaris. Ethiopia was still a strictly feudal country in as much as the king (Haile Selassie) appointed provincial governors in return for a payment. They, in turn, let out subsidiary jobs for a payment and so on. The most profitable job was the customs officer at the borders.

The British Consul told us he was responsible to the king for law and order in the whole of Southern Ethiopia. The country was very backward and the roads were awful; just tracks.

It took three days to drive to Addis Ababa on tracks through the bush. We had maps but they were almost totally useless. The Sandford family lived there. They had lived in Ewhurst during the war and we had gone to children's parties with their children. Brigadier Sandford had led the force that pushed the Italians out of Ethiopia and restored Haile Selassie to the throne in 1943.

We had a great time in this very simple capital city. Five Sandford children were working in various jobs in Addis. Through them, we met Bob and Mary Cameron who became very good friends later back in England. He was the Blackwood Hodge representative. They were friends of the ambassador who was away but his wife was very much in evidence and was great fun. I tried to get our £100 back at the Treasury but after much argument, I was shown a huge safe that was opened and it was pointed out that there was no money. It was the wrong time of the month, and government revenues were not due for a few weeks yet. We were going to have an audience with Haile Selassie but at the last moment, it was cancelled so we never met Rasta.

We left Addis towards the north into wonderful hilly and mountainous country. We were going to spend a night with Brigadier and Mrs Sandford who lived on a farm given them by the grateful king/emperor. We turned off the main road north and went about forty miles to this remarkable place. Perched on a cliff, the house was made of mud with whitewashed walls inside. By the house was a temperate farm with red poll cattle and fields of oats and barley. We then rode on a mule down a steep path to a different climate, much warmer and tropical vegetation. There, oranges, lemons and coffee were growing. There was a view from the house up this valley, which was, of course, part of the Rift, which was sensational. The old couple loved seeing us and, of course, remembered us as small boys.

We then drove north to Asmara in Eritrea, which was at the time administered from Addis. On the way, we deviated to Lake Tana, the source of the Blue Nile and a very ancient Christian church. Asmara was much more modern than Addis with a distinct Italian influence.

Then, towards the Sudan. Here we got off the main track through what was now sandy desert and crossed the border without knowing it. Suddenly we were surrounded by vehicles threatening to shoot if we did not stop. We were escorted back to Eritrea where we were put with our vehicle in a compound at the local prison. They were very hostile and made us unload everything from the Land Rover. They found our rifle and revolver and took these together with our ammunition.

Two days later we convinced them we had no money. We used to send money to the offices of Mitchell Cotts and our money was now in Khartoum. They let us go and we set off for Kassala on the Nile. Here we reported to the district commissioner's office where we were received by an immaculate Sudanese officer in khaki drill uniform who offered us tea. He told us he had taken over from his British predecessor, who had retired to Cobham in England. Indeed, he had been staying with him a few months ago.

Did we know Cobham? he asked. We said we did but not his predecessor. He then asked whether we would like to meet the chief of the Fuzzy Wuzzys after asking us whether we knew our Kipling. We said yes and so he shouted out of his window across a yard area full of people in white jalebis and was answered by a young man who came round to the office. Like the commissioner, he spoke perfect English and it transpired he had been at Cambridge a year ago.

On our way to Khartoum, we realised the clutch on our Land Rover was wearing badly so when we arrived, we got Mitchell Cotts to order us a new clutch assembly from Nairobi. We had to wait a week for this to arrive in Khartoum in the Grand Hotel. This was on the banks of the Nile where the blue and white merge.

It was one of the nastiest hotels in what we reckoned was one of the nastiest places in the world. There were no restaurants as we know it and the food in the hotel was awful. The only interesting thing was the boat traffic on the river. We had an interesting lunch with the ambassador who was in pretty rough temporary quarters while the embassy was being redone.

We set out for Atbara on the Nile from Khartoum, not having replaced the clutch as all seemed well again.

Halfway, there was a bang and we could only go in second gear. We limped into Atbara and found railway workshops as it was a railway centre and junction. Mercifully, we had the new spare clutch but changing the clutch on this model of Land Rover was an awful job. We had to remove the engine entirely to get at it, put the new clutch in, and replace the engine. We had a very comprehensive toolbox and a complete workshop manual. We borrowed a chain hoist to lift the engine and completed the job in two days. That clutch took us to England and lasted until the vehicle died of old age at North Breache Manor.

Our next stop was Wadi Halfa on the border with Egypt. There, we had to put the Land Rover and ourselves on a boat to Aswan as sand storms had obliterated the road north. From Aswan, we drove to Luxor where we booked into a hotel. The whole place was empty of tourists.

We hired a guide and went across the Nile to the Valley of the Kings where our very attentive guide showed us everything he could. On the way back, he said something about Germany or Germans assuming we were German. We put him right and said we were from England without thinking that, of course, it was only three years since we had bombed Egypt in 1956 during the Suez crisis.

With that, he hugged us tight and started shouting, 'The English are back!' We were led around the souk and welcomed by everyone. It was very moving.

Next, we drove north and spent two days in Cairo. I was keen to see where I had been in the army so we drove to Ismailia on the Suez Canal. As we were there, we drove to Suez and camped the night near Bir Odeib where we had the Irish Guards rest camp.

We then went back up the canal to Port Said and across the Nile Delta to Alexandria. Next stop was Libya, Benghazi, Tobruk, where there were some wonderful ruins, and then Tripoli. Faisal was king of Libya. It was very cold at night and we were very short of money so we camped only to find our water frozen in the morning.

We got as far as Tunis to be told the border with Algeria was closed as there was fighting. We booked ourselves and our Land Rover on a ferry to Marseilles. It was very rough and everyone was seasick except us so we had a good time. We drove more-or-less non-stop through France to Dover, took the ferry and arrived home three days before

Christmas 1959. We had been away for two years and three months, had a wonderful adventure, had seen a lot of the world, and got on pretty well, considering my brother and I are very different. We were both ready to settle down. We were done with travelling for the time being.

PART II

STOCKBROKING AND THE CITY

*O*n Boxing Day, I ran into Julia Calvert at a local drinks party. She asked me to dinner with her parents near Horsham in three days' time.

There were four Calvert girls and it was a large dinner party. At the end of dinner, Julia's father Robbie Calvert asked me to join him at the top of the table and questioned me about what I had been doing and what I might do now. I said I was looking for a job but if I did not find one, I might well go back to Australia.

To cut a long story short, on 7th January 1960, I started with L. Messel & Co stockbrokers in Throgmorton Street. Robbie was one of the senior partners and perhaps my father's connections in the City and industry had some reason for the offer of the job.

New recruits to stockbrokers usually spent up to the first year, learning how the office worked by spending time in the contracts department, then settlements, and even personnel. Luckily for me, the latter months of 1959 had been very busy and the office was overwhelmed trying to catch up and so I was sent to the research department under an extraordinary man Hugh Bowden-Smith.

I was paid a pittance of £250 a year and worked alternate Saturdays, which stopped fairly quickly. I got commission on any business I brought in. I think I was a quick learner but within months he had taught me to look at and fully understand company accounts, yields, P/E ratios and why one share might be cheaper than another.

They also discovered I could write quite well, which might have owed something to all those letters written from Australia and Africa. After some nine months, I avoided the general office altogether and went into the partners' room where I assisted the man who looked after Robbie Calvert's private clients.

My next break came when Messel hired Peter Riviere who was an expert in the short-dated gilt-edged or government stock, fixed-interest market with a life of five years or less. A number of men were interviewed to be his assistant but he chose me. I would be calling on Discount Houses and banks and dealing on the floor of the stock exchange. This meant I had to be a member of the stock exchange, which Messel arranged and paid for.

I worked for Peter for a year, which was enormous fun. He was ten years older than me, married but wild. His father had died at forty of a heart attack and he was sure the same would happen to him so life was for living. The gilt-edged market had a serious reputation for drinking and at 11.30 or 12 we'd adjourn to the Angel Court Club for the first gin and tonic.

Working in this market I had to wear a top hat as all the directors of Discount Houses did too.

These institutions no longer exist but nearly all of some ten were quoted companies. They soaked up the liquid funds of the banks on a daily basis and invested the money in trade bills and short-dated gilts, which they actively traded and that is where we came in.

One of those I called on was young but older than me, Jeremy Morse. I met up with him again later when he was chairman of Lloyd's Bank and we were both on the Council of Lloyds, the insurance market. My role was to tell him what was going on in the financial markets. However, he would tell me! I rapidly got bored with the monotony of the job and realised the drinking culture was not doing me much good when allied to socialising at night.

When I started at Messel, I met up with Jeremy Durham Matthews, who had been a fellow Irish Guardsman and flatmate. He was working at Lloyds and looking for someone to share a flat. We rented a two-bedroom flat with two bathrooms in Troy Court at the far end of Kensington High Street.

One of our entertainments was dog racing at the White City. Jeremy had a half-sister who had been set up in a flat by her father, Johnnie Moore but had gone off the rails with an infamous boyfriend called Edward Langley. She was obviously out of control and started to buy things at Harrods and Peter Jones, putting them on her mother's account, which could be done at that time.

Her father wanted to make her a ward of the court but was told by the judge he had to get her home. If she then ran away, he could come back to court and his request would be granted. The only trouble was he did not know where she was in London. He put a private detective onto the task of finding her.

We had been greyhound racing and got back to Troy Court at about 9.30 one night when Jeremy's stepfather, Johnnie Moore, rang in a high state of excitement to say his daughter Mary June was in the Cadogan Hotel in Sloane Street. We must go and get her and bring her home to Sussex. This was the summer of 1961. We jumped into our cars, Jeremy, me, and Billy Stanier who was back from Canberra, together with my girlfriend Vivienne Gorges and Billy's girl Rosie Pole Carew.

At the Cadogan Hotel, Jeremy gave £5 to the hall porter who confirmed Miss Moore was upstairs in her room. He telephoned to say Mr Langley was waiting for her in the lobby. There was one lift where Jeremy and Billy waited while I positioned myself on the stairs behind a huge vase of flowers. She elected to come down the stairs at which, I swooped, grabbed her kicking and screaming, and carried her out to

Jeremy's car where I dumped her in the back where Rosie who was a big girl sat on her.

Jeremy drove her home and delivered her to her father. He celebrated while she went to bed, got up long before him, climbed out of the window and made her way back to London. There she consulted a lawyer, John Cope, who said she had an open and shut case for assault.

Nevertheless, she was instantly made a ward of the court and so the Harrods and Peter Jones accounts were safe.

However, Jeremy and I were served with summons at our homes to appear at Bow Street Magistrates Court and Billy who was still a serving soldier had his served at the Guards Club, which caused a lot of merriment but some problems for him.

Johnny was mortified and said he would hire the finest barrister in the land to defend us, which he did in the person of Fred Lawton who was the George Carman of his day and finished his career as a Law Lord.

The trial at Bow Street in front of the Chief Magistrate Paul Bennett VC lasted three days and was widely reported. We were termed 'upper-class teddy boys' in a two-page spread in the *News of the World*. We were found guilty, given a discharge, and massive costs awarded, which naturally were paid by Johnnie Moore. At the end of the trial, John Cope, who had been prosecuting counsel, left court, went to the Chelsea register office, and married my cousin who happily, I did not know at all.

At this time, Jeremy and I wanted to be closer to civilisation and so we found a very nice maisonette in Cadogan Gardens near Sloane Square. It was a question of buying a lease. We tossed and I won and so Jeremy bought the lease. He had the large bedroom and I had the small one.

While my job was dealing in gilt-edged, I had started to get involved in dealing in equities for myself and the small trusts I had and for friends, making myself a bit of commission.

As 1961 came to an end, I decided I wanted to move on. David Stapleton told me he had been interviewed by a small firm, WI Carr, and was thinking of accepting a job offer from them. He knew they were looking for another person on a similar basis and suggested I call them up and say I was interested. It helped I was already a member of the stock exchange, which David was not but surprisingly they hired both of us to set up an operation dealing with institutions.

We started in early 1962. The senior partner was Commander Monkey Sellar RN who had commanded a destroyer in the war and had two DSOs and two DSCs. He had also captained England at rugby and played cricket for England in South Africa as well as captaining Sussex. He knew little or nothing about stocks or shares but there was not a door he could not open.

He took David and I round to one institution after another and left us to it. We were allowed to hire a rather clever economist Roy Crabbe who found ideas for us; and friends at the jobbers were happy to offer us shares to place. We also had friends who were managing shares and could direct business to us. David was very pushy and did a hard sell. I was rather different and a bit gentler. The clients fell into two camps. There were those who liked David and those who did not but liked me.

We then had an idea and hired another economist. When a company announced its results, usually in the afternoon after the market closed, our economists analysed them and produced a one-page commentary that we then sent round by messenger to all our institutional clients. It could then be on their desks when they arrived in the morning. In those days, the only real regular commentary on company results was the Lex column in the Financial Times. Often, we were in agreement with them but when we had spotted something Lex had not, there was scope for us to do good business.

It was a very exciting year. The partners did not think we would do much business and so they said we could have 15% of whatever we grossed in commission to divide equally between us. In the year ending April 1963, our first year, we grossed a bit over £400,000 so each of our bonus was £30,000 to add to our £1500 salary. That was about £750,00 in today's money. We were promptly made partners and encouraged to hire more people.

We had to modify the bonus arrangements a little as the partnership had, after all, met the cost of our economists and the messengers.

One of the first things I did was go to Christopher's, run by Peter Noble and buy a Pipe of Port, actually a hogshead of Graham 60 and a hogshead of Dow 60: about 650 bottles. I also bought myself a little house at 29 Graham Terrace, off Eaton Terrace; a thirty-year lease cost £5000. It had two bedrooms, a bathroom, a long living room, and a basement kitchen and dining room. It also had a small additional bedroom and a gents by the entrance to a small garden. It cost me £1000 to do up as the floor in the basement was earth and the long living room was created by removing a wall. It had two drawbacks as a house. The Underground from Victoria to Sloane Square went very close by and each time a train passed there was a rumble. Also, the water pressure was very poor so it took some time to run a bath. However, it was luxurious.

The necessity for my move was Jeremy D-M got married to Joanna Hoare in 1962 and so I had to move out of Cadogan Gardens, which was Jeremy's.

While doing up Graham Terrace, I lived at 13 Eaton Terrace, which was a large house inhabited by a mass of people who I knew, including John Morogh-Bernard, Denis Harvey Kelly, Rocky Petre, Billy Stanier, Peter Barclay and a number of other passers-through. Living in the basement was Ibrahim who had been our officers' mess cook in Egypt. He cleaned and did a bit of cooking for not much pay. He had suddenly arrived in England and through the regiment had found his way to 13 Eaton Terrace.

One weekend, the residents arrived back in the evening to find Ibrahim had fallen or jumped from the top floor through a glass roof and onto the kitchen floor – very messy and dead.

When my house was ready, a friend, Jimmy Coxon who had been in the regiment in Egypt and now worked at Rothschilds and gave me quite a bit of business, took the other bedroom in return for some rent.

He was very social and had a long walk out with the actress Susanna York. Domestically, he was not so good and I used to find him in bed eating scrambled eggs and bacon or baked beans out of the saucepan. He did not stay long as he got married.

Charlie Petre then took his place until he married Melanie Hoare and left. At that stage, I decided to live on my own and in advertising for a cleaner, I found Mrs Cuniffe. She was in her fifties, very Irish, and was looking for somewhere to live. I hired her as my housekeeper, and she lived in the tiny room on the way to the garden and abluted in the equally small gents. I was perfectly happy for her to use the bathroom when I had gone to work. She had a part-time job as a sort of companion to Lady Ravensdale who was Oswald Moseley's mother to whom she went four days a week.

The arrangement suited me fine. She used to cook me breakfast and would cook simple food for a dinner party or when I was in or with a girlfriend. She made a particularly good Irish stew. She had known better days and had a very pretty daughter who was grown-up but came to visit from time to time. She was a keen member of the Irish Club in Eaton Place. She cleaned and looked after the house. I was the envy of my friends

On returning from Australia, Michael Boyle asked me whether I would like to come and crew on his 12-metre again, the one in that Fastnet Race. She was now fully rigged as a 12-metre, had new sails and winches, and would be racing in the summer of 1960 with a number of other 12-metres; Flica 2 owned by Tony Boyden, Norsaga owned by Lord Craigmile, Evaine owned by Guy Lawrence, and Kaylena owned by my father's great friend Reggie Macdonald-Buchanan.

Also sailing would be Sceptre, now owned by Scotsman Eric Maxwell, but which had been built by the Royal Yacht Squadron (RYS) and had challenged for the America's Cup in 1959 but been soundly thrashed by the Americans.

From May through to August 1960, we sailed every weekend with a large party ashore and at sea. Some of us stayed on board. We would go down by train or car to Southampton and ferry to Cowes on a Friday evening and return on Sunday evening, having raced on Saturday and Sunday. Michael had been elected a member of the RYS

in Cowes and so we had parties there and if there were unoccupied rooms, some of us were able to stay as Michael's guests. Ladies were only allowed into a small sitting room but we could have a table and dinner there.

Vanity was not very successful as she was the oldest by far of the boats racing, circa 1921 or 22. Sceptre, ably sailed by Eric Maxwell and the newest boat, won most races. After sailing on Sunday, those of us driving would stop at Ashe Park for dinner where Michael Boyle lived and entertained on a grand scale. He was still a soldier in the Irish Guards with his servant Hamilton resplendent in livery as butler, at Ashe near Basingstoke.

In 1961, Michael bought a second 12-metre from the Labour politician Sir Hartley Shawcross.

This was a more modern boat and much more competitive. We assembled a good crew, which was principally Michael Boyle and Alan Burn or Mickey Boyd as helmsmen; Bill Walters on the main (a much older, lovely ex-Irish Guard who was large and very strong); Geoffrey Glanville as navigator and his twin Trevor on the foredeck; Hugh Lawson and myself on the winches amidships with two others; Loudie Constantine and Sir Geoffrey Shakerley on the foredeck. We were the hard core but when we were absent there were others to take our place as the old Vanity was in commission and other guests of Michael and the girls sailed on her.

Michael had a wonderful skipper, Albert Pengelly, and another younger man, George. In August, a number of the 12-metres went up to the Clyde where we sailed at Rothesay. In one race, we got into irons and were going sideways with the cockpit filling with water. Knives had to be used to cut sheets and we went upright again and then had to bale vast amounts of water out.

We generally behaved rather badly in the Glen Burn Hotel. Reggie Macdonald-Buchanan had come up to sail Kaylena. His formidable wife arrived a day or so later. She was unpacking when we all heard a loud shout from her of 'Reginald!' She had found a black lacy bra in a drawer and was blaming him. It was not a very likely scenario and he said he knew nothing about it, which was definitely true.

Bill Walters was very large and strong with a moustache. He had been a wartime soldier in the Irish Guards and spent most of the war in what he called the bag, prison camp. He sat on a table that collapsed and was summoned to the office of the under-manager to explain why he should not pay for it. The under-manager was sitting at his desk and was told by Bill to stand up when you address me.

'Why should I stand up for you? I am just as good as you.'

Bill retorted, 'No you are not, otherwise you would not be the under-manager of the Glenburn Hotel.'

On the way back to Cowes, we called into Dublin where we raced in Dublin Bay and then had an amazing party at the Royal Irish Yacht Club. Mongo Park came and sailed with us. I am afraid I did not do the trip to Scotland but I was told there was some incompetent navigation in as much as they found themselves sailing up the Bristol Channel rather than the Irish Sea and had to turn around and go back around St David's Head. I did the sail to Dublin but then flew back to work.

The following year, we set off to France in Vanity V. In the middle of the Channel, I fell through a hatch that someone had opened. I broke my right wrist quite badly so we turned around and returned to Cowes. We had no engine and so had to sail. We also turned the ensign upside down, which someone said was a distress signal. We were looking for someone with a motorboat to take me ashore and to hospital. We were later told that people who saw us thought we were probably all drunk as we did have a certain reputation. Anyhow, we got to Cowes and then Ryde hospital where they set my wrist. They did it very well but years later, I developed arthritis in it and had to give up squash and tennis.

1962 brought more excitement as Tony Boyden had decided to challenge for the America's Cup. He had commissioned a new 12-metre Sovereign. A few months later, two Australians, the Livingstone Brothers, and Own Aisher agreed to build another new 12-metre, Kurrewa, as a stalking horse.

The boats were launched around July, and I volunteered to be a crew on Kurrewa and was accepted to be in charge of pulling the sails up and down. We did a bit of practice sailing and all went well with both boats. Sovereign was crewed by Tony Boyden's Flica crew who were Harlequins Rugby Club with two or three internationals among them and Peter Scott as the helmsman. He had been a champion dingy man as well as world gliding champion, naturalist, and artist.

Early in the season, we had invited Prince Philip to come and helm Vanity V in a race. He brought Peter Scott, the famous naturalist and painter, with him as navigator. We were doing well and just about leading the fleet when we hit Ryde Sands. Many of us had not heard such blue naval language from the prince directed at the unfortunate Scott. We floated off quickly but had lost a lot of ground.

The following May, the two 12s were being shipped to Newport USA for the America's Cup races. I was asked to go with Kurrewa and so I formed up to my partners and asked whether I could take six weeks off to go to the USA to sail in the America's Cup. I was sharply told that is not why they had made me a partner. So, no America's Cup for Nutting.

In 1963, my brother Nick got married to Callie, a hard-riding and drinking girl from Gloucestershire. They had a grand London wedding at St Michael's Chester Square and I was best man. The family were a bit unsure about her but she turned out to be an excellent farmer's wife when my brother bought a farm in Somerset.

SOCIAL LIFE TITBITS UP TO 1964

On return from Africa and joining Jeremy Durham Matthews in the flat in Troy Court in Kensington High Street, I first made contact with Dawn Kettlewell who I had stolen from my brother! I had a number of fun weekends with her in Oxford where she lived but she then got engaged and that was the end of that.

I then met Vivienne Gorges who had a glamorous mother and a father who lived in South Africa. She worked for a theatrical agency, which meant she came across a number of interesting people. One evening, we found ourselves with Warren Beatty where I had my first experience of drugs. We smoked allegedly high-quality grass but it had no effect on me.

Vivienne's uncle was General Tremlett who lived at the Vine, a National Trust House. We spent happy times there but many more happy times with Michael Boyle at Ashe Park.

She had a first cousin Desmond Gorges who was obviously gay and was very amusing. He had an equally amusing friend Billy Hamilton, also gay who was loved by older women, including Maureen, Marchioness of Dufferin, and Ava.

One evening Billy Hamilton asked me whether I would make up a four for bridge with a friend of his, Stephen Ward, in whose mews house we would be playing. I cannot remember the fourth person but Ward was a bit creepy. He was also a very well-known osteopath with lots of grand clients including, it was alleged, Prince Philip.

While we played, there were two very young pretty girls who obviously lived there and who got us drinks when asked. Little did I know, I was in the company of Stephen Ward, Christine Keeler, and Mandy Rice-Davies. That was the only time I went there but a year or so later it was a grand scandal when Stephen was charged with living off immoral earnings. I wanted to volunteer as a witness for the defence but was very firmly told not to get involved. To this day I believe he was innocent but the government and police were out to get him. In particular, one was aware at that time the Met Police was riddled with corruption.

Another good friend of Vivienne's was Tim Philips; a very highly regarded painter who had studied under Annigoni and also Salvador Dali. I met the latter on two occasions and found him eccentric, borderline on mad. Annigoni had a studio in Pembroke Gardens as did Tim Phillips. We went there for dinner from time to time. One evening, Annigoni was very drunk. He tried to do the trick of removing the table cloth without breaking anything. It went disastrously wrong and there was a ghastly mess of broken china and glass.

Tim did a nude painting, back view lying on a chaise longue, of Vivienne, which he thought was one of his best works. It hangs in my dressing room to this day. It was relegated there when I got married!

At one stage, Vivienne and I got engaged. We told all our friends and our parents who were all rather surprised. We never put it in the paper and both of us agreed it would be a mistake and called it off within a week or so. Vivienne went off to Paris as she thought she needed some fresh air.

In 1962, casino gambling was legalised. I was a member of a new night club, Annabelles in Berkeley Square. Michael Aspinall who was famous for previously running illegal gambling, established the Clermont Club upstairs as a very exclusive casino. I joined and enjoyed playing Chemin de Fer with people much richer than me, including Greek shipowners, Lord Derby and the odd Arab. Lord Lucan played for the house. I survived in this company as I stuck to a strict rule I stopped when I had lost £100 and also when I was up £200. After a bit of time, I was up over £1000 but then I went to dinner, onto drinking and then to the Clermont. I lost at least £1000 and was mortified when I realised what I had done. I have never since gambled in a casino and never been a betting man since then. It was a very useful lesson as a young man.

Sara Curtis then came back into my life and we went out for over a year again. Then Susie Murray, who had lovely parents in Wiltshire, came into my life but she was already involved with a friend, Julian Bower, who she soon agreed to marry. I also met Bridget Holt who was American and had been a very successful model in New York. She had a mews house off Eaton Square. She had been married to a Woolworth heir who turned out to be gay so she was a bit fragile.

Some years later, after Poppity and I were married, she got engaged to James Rich, an American who was the heir to the Simoniz car-polish fortune. She asked me to give her away, which I did by marching her down the aisle at Farm Street Church. We had a small reception at Pembroke Road. They went off on honeymoon to Greece and he went off before a week was out. Allegedly, he needed to get married to break a trust. She came back swearing she would take him for everything he had.

I took her to see Derek Clogg, at that time the leading divorce lawyer in London. To her great disappointment, he told her the courts were unlikely to give her anything very much for a week's marriage.

MORE SAILING (1962–1964)

I had got very much hooked on sailing, rather to the exclusion of other sports and activities. 12-metre sailing continued into 1963 but I also got involved in ocean racing. Neil Watson, who was a godfather to Susie Murray, a girlfriend, asked me to join his crew on Springtime, a 42 ft yawl. We were at the top of Class Two and had a good crew. Neil navigated. Alastair Easton, a yacht broker, ex-navy Commander Easton took one watch and I usually took the other one. Our crew included Jonathan Bradbeer and two Rogers brothers who became very successful racing all over the place a few years later. We did a North Sea race from Harwich to Hook of Holland, two Dinard races, the Channel Race just before Cowes, the Fastnet Race in 1963 and the La Rochelle race in 1964 as well as others.

In the summer of 1962, Tony Boyden built another 12metre Sovereign, which he proposed to take to America for a challenge in 1964. We raced against her and Sceptre but rarely got near them.

In the summer of 1963, Michael Boyle got married. We had a bachelor party in the Mikado Room in the Savoy Hotel. There were about twenty for dinner. After dinner, Michael climbed onto the table to tell some stories. In the process, he picked up a plaster-of-Paris table decoration with a long handle and swung it around his head. The handle broke and the decoration struck me on the head. I bled profusely from the wound and so Alan Burn and Bill Walters took me over to the Charing Cross Hospital, which was then just over the road.

When I came out from being stitched up, six or seven stitches and a scar to this day, I found Burn and Walters whizzing each other up and down the hospital corridor on a trolley.

We finished the 1963 season as Michael was then posted to Germany in the army and so he sold old Vanity. Vanity V was taken over by Loudie Constantine, Hugh Lawson and me but not really raced in 1964. We did take her to Deauville. She had no engine and so we had to sail down the narrow passage into the harbour when the tide was in, down sails and spin her round to halt. We used the tender with outboard motor to facilitate this. We went racing in Deauville and some of us stayed in the Normandie Hotel.

In 1963, I came into the morning room in the RYS Castle and found Reggie Macdonald-Buchanan there. He asked how my father was and then said I always seemed to be in the Castle so I should become a member. I said that would be very nice. He promptly organised it with him as proposer, Michael Boyle's father, Commander Patrick Boyle as seconder and support from Philip Colville who sailed Dragons, Bill Burnham, Hugh Lawson's elder brother and my Irish cousin Mungo Park. With that slate and being unknown, I was duly elected at the Cowes week meeting in 1964 together with Hugh Lawson, Charles de Selincourt and Sir Ernest Kleinwort.

I was playing the field as far as the opposite sex was concerned but started seeing quite a bit of Fiona Fairfax, She had been Michael Boyles' secretary and organised all his parties. She had a low gravelly voice, was herself a party girl and was very good company.

In June 1964, she got a job running Continental Villas. This was a business owned by Ronnie Andgel, Nick Leche, who had been at WWW with me, and Geoffrey Johnston. They managed villas in the south of France, which they rented out to people. Fiona was hired as head girl and had the run of empty villas. Also, in Eze, Antibes and St Tropez, they had hired a number of girls to look after the villas, meet the guests, shop for them and clean when they had gone. They were provided with the most rudimentary and cheap accommodation that could be found and paid a pittance but they were in the south of France.

Fiona suggested I came down to stay. I brought my friend David Darling and we drove down in my brown Mercedes, towing a tin boat and outboard on a trailer. Apart from the wheel of the trailer coming off on the Route N7 at 100 mph, we arrived safely. The accident happened just outside a garage and workshop who repaired the wheel, new bearing, etc. In Eze, we met up with Henry Seymour and Christopher Stockdale. After a few days there, we moved on to Antibes with Fiona. There she announced that she had to go to St Tropez the following day. There were about five very pretty girls in St Tropez and she had told them we men would take them out to dinner.

We would meet the girls in Seneques on the front in St Tropez. Seymour and Stockdale got very drunk in a bar playing pool for money and did not turn up. When we got there, there were indeed five pretty girls but one was small with long blond hair and just about the prettiest face I had ever seen. She was dressed all in pink. We went to dinner and she sat next to me, which is when I discovered she was not a dumb blond but had lots to say for herself. We went on to a nightclub and spent the next few hours together before stumbling back to her lodgings, which were pretty primitive but we both collapsed on a reasonably sized bed.

I was captivated and we spent the next day on the beach but with lots of others around. I had to leave for home the next day. I returned in August for a few days with the car and boat but left the car and boat with Fiona. We had a plan for her to drive it to Rome where I would meet her with my mother and then take my mother to Elba.

I should explain. My father had died in March, actually when I was in Paris at Colin Clive's wedding. I flew back immediately but was too late. He had been ill for many years and still went to work when he could. He had a number of hideous operations to sort out hardening of the arteries. He lost a toe that had gone gangrenous. He was gassed twice and had terrible dysentery during WWI. He smoked forty cigarettes a day throughout his life and a pipe. Of course, he would have had a heart bypass some years later, which would probably have prolonged his life. My mother had a terrible time with him but she adored him.

Anyhow at the end of September, my mother and I flew to Rome, met up with Fiona and the car and boat. We did Rome for a day and then drove up to take the ferry to Elba. Thence to a charming hotel in a bay where we launched the boat.

We spent a very happy ten days meeting up with Hillary Lawson/Burnham and her sisters having a break away from their husbands. Fiona and I water-skied and my mother loved it. We then flew back leaving car and boat with Fiona who would return it in a week's time.

I had said to the pretty blond in pink, Poppity Russell, call me when you get back from the south of France as I don't know how to call you. I had only been back a few days at the beginning of October when the telephone rang in Graham Terrace and it was Poppity.

POPPITY

*S*he was only twenty-one but the eldest of six. Her parents were Cosmo and Agnes Russell. He had been with the Council of Europe in Strasbourg so Poppity had been educated in France up until then. He was a brilliant linguist, speaking numerous European languages. He was currently working in PR in London but a few years later, he returned to Brussels as a translator.

I immediately took her out to dinner and then took her down to North Breache to meet my mother who was enchanted. I had collected her from Dorking Station on Saturday morning. On arrival, my mother took her into the dining room where there was the drinks cabinet and asked her what she would like to drink. Whiskey and soda she said to my mother's surprise. She later said she could not think what she wanted but it was the first thing that came into her head.

Two weeks later, we discovered our birthdays were on the same day, 22nd October, so I organised a party at Graham Terrace. I had already decided she was going to be my wife and so after our first brief meeting in the south of France in June, even briefer meeting in August and about four weeks of seeing a lot of each other, I proposed we got married.

I think Poppity was understandably stunned. She refused to give me an answer but a few days later caved in and said yes. I had never met her parents and only her brother Nick at a cocktail party. We drove down to Rye where her parents lived in a charming but very scruffy house outside Rye. All the two brothers and three sisters were there to see this extraordinary man who was going to marry their sister. By this time, Poppity had got herself a job selling Cindy Dolls in Selfridges on commission and was earning over £150 per week. She had to work Saturday Mornings and so she came down on the train afterwards. We had a small shoot on the farm and one Saturday, I was late meeting the train which was very unpopular. We fixed the date of the wedding on 31 March 1965.

BUSINESS DEALINGS

*O*n the business front, I had got involved with Casa Pupo, which had a large shop in the Pimlico Road selling rugs, glass, and china from Spain. The business was run by Geoffrey Dobson and his gay partner Jose Casasus who was very artistic. I invested a small amount of money in 1961 and then my friend Julian Earle who was the major shareholder wanted to retire to the south of France and so he sold me his shares in 1964, which made me the controlling shareholder with about 40%.

I had also made an investment in a business making stretch covers for furniture with my friend David Darling, and I became chairman of his company. David was working for and with Arthur Carrington who had a jacquard circular-knitting business in Market Harborough, which made the fabric for stretch covers. We eventually put the two businesses together as Welland Textiles. We installed a computer and then employed as our computer manager Elvin Patrick who came back into my life many years later as the boss and very successful underwriter of a large syndicate at Lloyd's.

Welland was a very successful business but we started to see competition from the biggest manufacturer of stretch covers, Custom-agic which was a quoted company. After much negotiation, we sold

Stretchova to Customagic for a large shareholding in that company and some cash. David Darling and I joined their board.

The company was run by two Linder brothers in Manchester and a cousin in London. Each of the three of them had a Rolls Royce and chauffeur and the chauffeurs each had a top of the range car, a Ford Granada. They lived the life of Riley on the company and there was an item in the management accounts, cigars. We rapidly fell out with them, made a real nuisance of ourselves and they agreed to buy back our shareholding on a very favourable basis to us. The stretch cover business was in decline.

C & C

*M*y father had a rather low opinion of stockbrokers but he had said he would try to find a way of putting me on the board of a company that made something when I had made a success of stockbroking. So, in 1963, I was appointed a director of C&C (C& C), which was the main operating company of E&J Burke Ltd which was quoted on the London and Dublin Stock Exchanges. The company had soft drinks factories at Southfields in London, Stockport near Manchester, and Kirkintilloch near Glasgow. It had a virtual monopoly in Northern Ireland, owned Smiths Potato Crisps, and a Schweppes factory in Dublin as it owned the Schweppes label in Ireland. It had a business importing citrus juices and another company that made the ingredients for all the soft drinks produced. It also owned 65% of A&R Thwaites, which owned Mineral Waters Distributors and the C&C labels in Southern Ireland.

Burkes was my grandfather's business and had been run by my father in the 1920s. My father was nominally chairman of Burkes but for many years had played no part in running the business. This was done by Bob Pinnock who was almost a contemporary of my father. In addition to me, there was Peter Ewen who was senior partner of the company's auditors and Thomas Swan – a solicitor who represented Walt Disney in England. Then there was Bob Rolston who ran the successful Northern Ireland operation. He was well-connected in Northern Ireland. An Australian, Max Phillips, was company secretary.

The company had agreed a deal with Courage brewers to form a joint venture based on the Southfields factory to supply Courage pubs with C& C soft drinks; tonic, bitter lemon, club soda, and ginger ale. Subsequently, it had been agreed to sell the Southfields factory, which was old, too small and on a site suitable for housing. This would enable the company to put up half the money for a new factory in Sunbury.

Then my father died in March 1964 swiftly followed by Bob Pinnock. This changed everything. Peter Ewen urged me to give up stockbroking and succeed my father but as executive chairman. He said Bob Rolston would make a splendid managing director. He and Tommy Swan would stay on and Max Phillips could become finance director. This is what rapidly happened and I found myself chairman of a fully listed company at twenty-eight years of age.

I went to my partners at WI Carr and they agreed I could remain a sleeping partner with my name on the writing paper. They would pay me a retainer of £1500 per year and 30% of the commission of any business.

I was giving up some £25,000 a year in return for that plus £6500 from Burkes. But I got a car paid for by Burkes, health insurance and inclusion in a pension scheme as well as generous expenses. I had none of these things at WI Carr. At this time, a wicked tax surtax took one's top rate up to nearly 90% and so I worked out I would be no worse off in reality.

Bob Rolston and I decided the small offices in Holborn were unsuitable and the lease was at an end.

We found a suite of offices in Pall Mall at Quadrant House at the bottom of St James's Street. It had a huge panelled board room into which we installed a board-room table and two partners desks one for me and one for Bob when he was in London. I also took a parking space under the Economist building. This was offered to members of the club, Boodles, which I had joined in 1960.

We had a lot to do. We had to finalise the arrangements with Courage on the basis we had control as it was our product the company was producing. We finished with a 60/40 deal, with Courage putting up half the cost of the new factory.

During the summer all the bottling-and-other plant was moved from Southfield to Sunbury. We then had to sort out Kirkintilloch, which was losing money. We closed the business down and supplied from Stockport, keeping a small distribution warehouse.

In May, I suddenly received a letter from the USA from Walter Mack, chairman of Great American Industries, which owned the C&C label in the USA. Walter had built ten plants in the US, largely financed by Continental Can Company, to produce canned soft drinks under the C&C label. He was interested to know whether we would like to import some of his product and invited me to visit New York. He had set the production lines in all his new plants going simultaneously by pressing a button in Atlanta, the HQ of Coca Cola., which cocked a snook at that company.

Walter had been CEO of Pepsi Cola during and after the war and was nearly eighty. Bob thought it would be interesting for me to go and meet these people and so, at the end of June, I flew to New York. I stayed at the St Regis Hotel, booked by Walter, and met him in his office high up in the Chrysler building.

We got on famously, despite me saying we would not import canned soft drinks from him. He had some good ideas about franchising and agreed to sell us some essence for his cola drink, which was rather better than ours. He had also invited me to the coming-out dance of his younger daughter and said I should bring white tie, which I did. The party at the St Regis was very American. Actually, I was either too old for the young or too young for the old but I danced with quite a lot of pretty girls.

Walter and Ruth Mack also took me to a first-night gala of *Hello*

Dolly. I met up with his son-in-law John Thomas who had recently joined the company from Princeton Law School. We became good friends and visited one of the canning plants in New Jersey. I also made contact with Burnham and Co who were WI Carr's correspondents in New York and through whom they did American business. We left with a promise from Walter to get Bob Fowler, a friend of his, to contact us. Bob had worked for Coca Cola and had set up all their franchises in Europe after the war.

Great American Industries was quoted on the American Exchange and was a conglomerate. It had a hugely profitable business in Bedford Virginia making neoprene and rubber bits and pieces such as the insulation around the windows of all Boeing aeroplanes. It had a mining division and the soft drinks business.

On my return, it was time for a bit of sailing. There were no more Vanitys and so Hugh Lawson and I offered our services to Lord Craigmyle on Norsaga. We thought we would have a change and said we would do the foredeck. This was a mistake as in each of the first two races we dropped the spinnaker in the water and were last. We were sacked!

I did a bit of Ocean Racing on Spring Time and then Fiona Fairfax and I agreed to help deliver a sailing boat for Richard Aykroyd to Lisbon. A friend, John Chandler, was the skipper as he was going to take the boat on to Majorca with another crew.

The Bay of Biscay was very rough and unpleasant and we put into Corunna to do some running repairs. We could not get away soon enough as there was a fish factory upwind and the smell was unbearable. When we arrived in Lisbon, we anchored off Cascais. There was a heatwave in Lisbon with temperatures over 100 F.

We tidied up the boat but could not wait to cool down in the water. I jumped in and it nearly stopped my heart as the water temperature was only about 50 degrees.

This was between trips to St Tropez. I had also found the time to visit Ireland again and meet all the C&C people as well as staying with Mungo Park, my cousin. In 1962, I had sailed with him on his sailing boat Kitugani in the waters off Cork.

We went into Schull where we met Paddy O'Keefe, a splendid old man who had his fingers in everything in that area. He also owned the pub in Schull as well as Castle Island off Schull in Roaring Water Bay, looking out at the Fastnet Rock. It was about 120 acres and had about eight ruined substantial houses as well as a huge jetty.

It was a glorious day and in a mad moment, we agreed to buy it from him for £3000. A substantial rowing boat came with it. This was kept in a very sheltered little bay with a jetty on the mainland that had a crossing to our jetty of about 300 yards. I put up 66% of the money. Our idea was to fly to Cork, keep a car there and drive down for a long weekend. Sadly, that never worked as Aer Lingus and BEA had a stranglehold on the route from London to Cork so the flights were always full.

Nevertheless, we got a builder in Schull to put up a wooden Colt House near the jetty and we found a good water supply. No loo but rather a spade! In 1963, I spent two long weekends there and took Sara on one and another girlfriend, Patricia Turner Edwards on another. It was wonderful.

After we were married in 1965, Pops and I joined Mongo and his family, Lorna his wife, and Tudi, Carolyn, and ghastly, badly behaved Mongo Junior together with Pops' sister Tinky and Mongo's boat for a week. It was definitely camping but the weather was good.

We fished, sailed and went to Bantry Bay and other places. We had rented a car at Cork airport. This was the last time we found the time to go back.

A local farmer used to swim about forty cattle over to the island, tying them to the side of his boat. He paid quite good money for the grazing.

A few years later, the problems in Ireland became very serious and Schull was a hotbed of IRA and so we did not want to go. However, in 1973, I was suddenly contacted by a Mr Langham, who lived in Kent. He wanted to buy Castle Island. We sold it to him for £12,000, which was a handsome profit. I never met him, and it was said he had never gone to the island but there was nothing wrong with his money.

GETTING MARRIED AND TAKING
CARE OF BUSINESS MATTERS

*B*ack in London, I was made chairman of Cantrell and Cochrane Southern the joint company with Courage. We negotiated a deal with Friary Meux and Fremlins whereby they took up shares and their managing directors joined the board. Burkes reduced to 51%.

In November, we were contacted by Schweppes and I was asked to go and see Viscount Harold Watkinson, the MD, at his offices in Connaught Square just off Marble Arch. He had been the minister for defence in the Conservative government under Harold Macmillan.

They owned a soft drinks business, Dewsbury and Brown, in Manchester which did not fit with their main business. He proposed that it should merge with our business in Stockport in a joint company. It was not a difficult negotiation. We finished with a 50:50 company. We moved our production to their bigger premises and sold our factory. We agreed the north of England and Scotland would be their territory and the company would sell C&C products as well as Dewsbury and Browns products. The expectation was two unprofitable businesses would make one profitable one.

We now had a strong relationship with Schweppes as, in addition, we owned their label in Ireland, which was a profitable business for us.

I then invited my cousin and great friend Mungo Park, who was senior partner of Dudgeons, the second-largest Dublin Stockbrokers, to become Chairman of Schweppes Ireland.

As we were preparing for our wedding on March 31, I had an unpleasant task at C&C Southern. It became apparent that the MD was not up to the job. The board were united in the view that he should be replaced by Griffith Kewley who was recommended by Courage. I met him, liked him and he was very different from the current MD.

As chairman, I had the difficult task of telling the MD he was being fired as we had lost confidence in him. He was in his mid-50s. It came as a bolt out the blue to him and he burst into tears. I felt a frightful shit but we agreed to terms, which I said I would put to the board.

A board meeting was scheduled for the first of April, which was the only day the Courage, Friary, and Fremlins people could do. I reluctantly agreed. It was not possible before our wedding and afterwards, we were going on our honeymoon to the Caribbean. So we were married on 31 March. The Burke board agreed to buy my brown Mercedes, and I was given a new company car a dark blue Mercedes.

I bought Poppity, as a wedding present, a white two-seater soft-top MG. We were married in the Guards Chapel by Pops' grandfather, Canon Parsons, and the chaplain of the Guards Chapel. We had a full orchestra from the band of the Irish Guards under the direction of Major Jigs Jaeger, the director of music who we had met up with in West Australia.

We then went to the Hyde Park Hotel for the reception. We had nearly 700 guests as by now I had a huge circle of people to ask from the stock exchange, the regiment, our family home, and now Burkes as well as family. Pops who was twenty-two had a huge family and a lot of friends from school. One of my first brushes with her father was his wish to seat on the bride's side of the church about 100 family members in order of precedence. He had it all written out. I told him it was impossible for the ushers to implement that. I think we compromised on about 30 in the first three pews.

My mother was wonderful, and Poppity's parents Cosmo and

Aggie, together with Pops and I, formed the receiving line. There we were when the man in a red coat flung open the doors and announced the first couple, 'Sir Marmaduke and Lady Strickland Constable.' One remembers little things like that. She was Pop's great aunt.

The first drama was the non-appearance of the senior member of the bride's family, Lord Ampthill, who had agreed to make the speech proposing our health. After a search, it was clear he was not there and so Cosmo stepped into the breach and did little more than propose our health. My brother as best man was pretty short, and I was equally so, and so the lack of speeches seemed to go down well.

We were going on to the Savoy where we had a suite booked for two nights. We were about twenty-five for dinner in the ballroom but Pops and I retired quite early. I had to get up in time to go to Sunbury to chair the C&C Southern meeting. Pops entertained in our suite.

As I walked back into the Savoy, the first person I saw was Pop's uncle Alaric Russell. He asked what on earth I had been doing. I replied that I had been to a board meeting. He was flabbergasted.

After lunch, we went back to Graham Terrace where Mrs Cunniffe was still in tears. She had been at the reception and poor David Darling had looked after and comforted her but she was well-refreshed.

THE HONEYMOON

*P*ops had already packed and so I finished mine as we were to fly to Antigua the following day. We spent a few days in The Inn at English Harbour and then picked up Flica. This was Tony Boyden's old 12-metre, which had been sold to John Clegg. He had converted her into a cruising boat for four passengers. We were two and in addition had John Clegg as skipper and cook, he had an Australian and a Canary Islander as crew.

We set sail southwards. There were few other yachts around. The first day Pops was a bit sick. It must have been the sea as it was too early for her to be pregnant. Pops had done very little sailing and so it was a baptism of fire. However, she very soon got over it and we visited some lovely bays, swam, and were wonderfully well-fed by John Clegg who was an excellent cook. One of the highlights was a dance or jump-up on Union Island. We were the only white people there and they all wanted to dance with Pops. It was a great evening.

We went ashore on Mustique. There was nothing there except a bit of a bog and lots of mosquitos. After just over two weeks we got to Grenada where we said goodbye to John and his crew. We meant to spend one night in a hotel before flying to New York where I had meetings arranged. In the event, we had to stay four nights as there were problems with flights. We got to see a lot of this lovely island as a result.

We then flew to Antigua, on to Miami and then to New York. We again stayed in the St Regis. Walter Mack was keen to show Pops New York. We also became friendly with Walter's oldest daughter who we discovered was married to John Thomas. They invited me to join the board of Great American Industries. I would be paid $1000 (the exchange rate then was nearer $4 to a pound) per board meeting attended and my expenses in doing so.

FINDING A HOUSE

*W*e were away for five weeks and it was a bit of a let down on return. Pops moved into Graham Terrace with me and Mrs Cuniffe moved out but continued to clean for us.

In July, David Parkes asked us to join him in Helsinki to sail across the Baltic to Stockholm. Joya was about 50 foot and a prewar, narrow, single-masted wooden sloop. David and his girlfriend Toni Clifford Wolf were debating whether to get married. We set off in lovely weather and sailed to the Aland Islands where we stopped for a very good lunch and were loaned the use of a sauna. In the late afternoon, we set off to sail to our next anchorage when the wind got up and it started to rain. In the Baltic, there is a complicated navigation system of lights, which works well until a light goes out. In heavy rain and strong wind, we crashed into a rocky island that should have had a light on it. We holed Joya and started to take in water. Pops and Toni manned the pump while David and I polled her off the rocks.

Nearby, we saw a sandy beach so we drove her up onto it until she was beached forward. We had a lot of water to pump out but David succeeded in cannibalising the hot water system into a pump, which kept the water down. The following morning we carried out repairs with me in the water. We waited for the wind to go down and the following day set off for Stockholm. We had bent the propeller shaft so we could not use the engine. The mast had also moved and looked pretty precarious.

I sat on the big tiller as we sailed up the Skattegat saying to myself, 'If the mast breaks, bear away.' If you don't, the mast comes down on top of you. We safely got to Stockholm and dry land was very welcome. After that adventure, which nearly put Pops off sailing, we decided we needed a family house so Pops started to look. We looked at all sorts of properties in mainly Kensington, including the Cambodian Embassy on Campden Hill.

Suddenly, in June, I got a call from Pops that I had to seriously come and see the most wonderful house she had found in Pembroke Road. It was a bit more than our budget but had to be worth it. 31 Pembroke Road was fantastic. It had a three-room basement flat, large drawing-room and dining room, small kitchen. On the first floor, there was a master bedroom, bathroom, dressing room, sitting room, a single bedroom, and another bathroom. On the top floor, there were two large rooms, a small room, and a big bathroom. There was a huge garden, running down to a double garage and gates opening on to Logan Place. There was room to park another car or two inside the gates.

The only problem was that it was way over our budget. I raised £25,000 on a mortgage and we bought it. Included were all the carpets, curtains and many fittings, which were in good order.

It was indeed a family house. We moved from Graham Terrace at the end of September and a few weeks later Pops was pregnant.

BUSINESS GOES ON

$\mathcal{M}$ eanwhile, business went on. I started to look at buying out the minority shareholders in Thwaites in Ireland so we could consolidate their profits with ours. The Bank of Ireland was willing to lend us the money, and so we then entered what turned out to be a very difficult negotiation. Eventually, the directors of Thwaites agreed to recommend and we bought out a mass of small shareholders, having to exercise compulsory purchase for the last 2 or 3%.

I was then appointed chairman of Thwaites, which was wholly owned by Burkes. In June, I had chaired my first annual general meeting (AGM) of Burkes in Dublin, which was now a large Irish company, with many shareholders and members of the press present. This was nerve-racking but went off quite well.

A bit later, a fascinating insight into Ireland at that time,1965-1966, occurred. We needed to beef up the finance side of the business and had the ideal candidate for promotion in Brennan Geddes. He was a chartered accountant and was running Schweppes Ireland. There was an obvious successor there. The only problem was that Geddes was a

Catholic and no Catholic had ever worked at the Thwaites HQ building on Kildare Street. All the Thwaites people were Protestants. The discussion had everyone prevaricating without mentioning religion. Eventually, Rex Dick, the MD of Thwaites said, 'Peter, it might be an idea if our colleagues would allow us to have a word next door in my office.' They agreed, and we left the meeting. He said I was probably not aware that Geddes was a Catholic and no Catholic had ever worked in this building. I said, I was totally aware of the problem but was it not time to change things? He agreed, we returned to the meeting and said we were aware of the precedents but thought it was time for change. Everyone agreed.

Bob Rolston was a sophisticated man but I remember him coming to lunch in London with his wife. He had returned from a motoring holiday in France and Italy where he had been at St Peter's Square at the Vatican on a Sunday and seen the Pope delivering his Sunday address. He said how impressed he had been. I was due to visit him in Belfast the following week. Before he left, he said to me that under no circumstances should I mention to anyone in the company that he had been to Rome. The company in N. Ireland only employed members of Orange Lodges and never had a Catholic darkened its doors.

The transport manager was a tough but charming individual. Many years later, Billy Carson emerged as a leading light in the Loyalist paramilitaries and did frightful things with an electric drill before being killed by the IRA.

In London, I took on David Hay in the London office to work on franchising our mixer range in Europe. He and I went to Vienna where he had found a company that agreed to take our essences and sell them under licence of the C&C label. We also went to Volvic where Thwaites had an arrangement to sell them essences but not under the C&C label. I don't think we converted them.

Dick Fowler, Walter Mack's friend, ex-Coca Cola, then joined us as a consultant with a deal where he would share in any profits from any deals he did. Through the good offices of Cosmo, Pops' father, whose PR company was the O'Brien Organisation, we went to see Vittel with Dick Fowler. Nothing came of this but I was offered the distribution rights for England for Vittel water. The only bottled water on sale in

England at that time was Malvern Water, owned by Schweppes, and I knew it was an unprofitable product. In England, you could drink the tap water but in the sixties in France, you could not, which was why they had all these bottled-water businesses. I turned the offer down, saying bottled water would never take off in England. How spectacularly wrong I was.

In the summer of 1966, I went to have lunch with Harold Watkinson at Schweppes, which was a regular occurrence. When I was shown into his office, he presented me with a letter from Kleinwort's, his merchant bankers, which amounted to a take-over offer for Burkes. He hoped we could do a friendly deal. I said I was bitterly opposed to any take-over at this moment. Our profits were slightly reduced as we had the cost of the loan to buy out the Thwaites minority and had write-offs and costs from the deals we had done. We had, conversely, not yet seen the benefits come through.

I took the letter back to the office after a rather frosty lunch, called the board, and had a meeting that evening. Peter Ewen was all for fighting any offer, but I was asked to contact Jacob Rothschild who I knew from school. I did so the following morning and he passed me on to Philip Shelbourne who was their top corporate partner.

We had a meeting with him and he was gloomy about resisting an offer because of our lower profits. He recommended we talked to Guinness as they might be persuaded to make a better offer. They did agree to make a better offer which made Schweppes make a better offer still. Guinness came back with a still better offer but had talked to Schweppes and if they were successful, they would sell the English businesses and Schweppes Ireland while keeping the Irish businesses. We had been stitched up but we had a very good price for the shareholders.

There were lots of meetings to iron things out and I learned a lot about corporate finance. At one meeting, the question of my future came up. I said I had no interest in a continuing role and so they said what did I want for my contract. I suggested a year's salary, which they readily agreed. But I did not have a contract and so that was a windfall of £6500.

By October, all was tied up. I said goodbye to my wonderful office and went back to WI Carr where I was welcomed with open arms. I soon picked up with my old clients and started to produce business.

It was a fortunate sale as following gaining control of Thwaites, we had agreed to sell two factories in the middle of Dublin and build a brand-new factory just outside Dublin. Just as that came on stream, there was a more-or-less general strike in Ireland and nothing was produced in the new factory for nearly a year. It would have broken us as a company but Guinness had the financial muscle to survive it.

DOMINICA

his all started in 1965 when C&C found that their subsidiary, Burkes Citrus Products, run by Eric Peters and importers of juices for us and other customers, was unable to supply us with lime juice. Ghana had bad civil unrest, Jamaica had suffered a hurricane, and Roses had Dominica tied up. These were the only three countries that grew sufficiently flavoured limes to make lime juice cordial.

We were contemplating cheating with lemon essence when Eric Peters came to see me in my office. He had a letter from a company in Dominica, offering to supply good quantities of lime juice. It was from a Mr Osborne who ran a company that purported to do a mass of different things. I suggested Peters went to Dominica immediately.

He came back and said Osborne was acting for a company owned by one of the leading families on the island, Shillingford. They had a factory processing limes but all their production traditionally had been sold to Roses, which was owned by Schweppes, and makers of Rose Lime Juice Cordial, who also had a factory and offices on the island. Peters offered a far higher price, which thrilled the Shillingford family and company.

A year later, messages then came back from Shillingford, asking whether we would like to buy into their company. At about this time,

John Ingledew, who had a business in Cardiff and lived in Monmouth –
I had met him when canvassing for Richard Yorke, a barrister and
friend who was the Conservative candidate in the general election, in
Durham – came to see me and said did I have any ideas about investments overseas as he hated this Labour government and would like to
get some assets abroad. I said the only thing possible was a crazy idea
of buying into a firm of general merchants in Dominica in the West
Indies. John's reaction was one of huge enthusiasm as he had spent
three months there some four years previously where his wife, Caroline's godfather was the chief medical officer. He had broken a leg and
was advised to go somewhere warm to recuperate.

So, in the summer of 1966, John and I set off for Dominica. We
were met at the airport on the Windward side of the island, after
spending a night at The Inn at English Harbour in Antigua where we
had been on our honeymoon. It was a dramatic landing down the side
of a mountain and out to sea into the Trade Winds. Dominica is 50
miles long and about 20 miles across but mountains down the middle,
covered in rainforest, go up to 4600 ft, which is higher than any in
the UK.

The road from the airport took us over the middle of the island
through jungle. It took about one-and-a-half hours to cover about 40
miles of twists and turns with steep gradients. We arrived in the capital, Roseau, and checked into the Fort Young Hotel, which was the
best and nearly only on the island.

The following day, Osborne took us off and tried to sell us two
estates growing mainly bananas but anything will grow in Dominica. In
the middle of the island, it rains every day with rainfall exceeding 350
inches per annum. It's much less on the coast but it's still a wonderful
climate for growing anything.

We were then introduced to Irving Shillingford, the elderly head of
the Shillingford family and chairman of AC Shillingford. The original
Shillingford was a seaman from Glasgow who settled on the island and
had 128 children by multiple women so, masses of people were Shilling-
fords. Irving was his eldest son and there were a number of the family
in the business. He explained to us that his great worry was that when
he was gone, which might be quite soon his family would wreck the

business by quarrelling. He was interested in the idea of selling a controlling interest to good people who would keep the business going and pay out the profits to the shareholders each year. The company needed money to develop and he envisaged us acquiring some 51% by subscribing new money.

It was an interesting proposition as the company had a headquarters building in the middle of Roseau with a supermarket on the ground floor together with a wholesale side. Upstairs was a shipping department dealing with imports and exports and acting for shipping lines, an insurance business, and the offices. They were agents for Bedford trucks, and there were a number of small shops in the town. They had a factory where the limes were processed as were cocoa and coconuts/copra. There was also an estate on the road to the airport of about 100 acres growing bananas, oranges, lemons, and limes as well as coconuts and especially grapefruit, which was a major crop on the island.

Our answer was that we were interested but we would want someone to come and check out the business and go through the accounts. On returning home, I was introduced to Francis Brown who had sorted out a business for Peter Cadbury in Tobago. He had been a CSM in the Coldstream Guards and an excellent middleweight boxer. He had been working for a small firm of management consultants. He readily agreed to go to Dominica at our expense to check out the business. His initial reports were pretty pessimistic but he made friends with the family in the business and came home to say he would like to go and live in Dominica and run the business.

Thus, in the Autumn of 1966, John, Francis, and I went out to Dominica. I had just completed the sale of E&J Burke to Guinness. We negotiated a deal whereby John and I each put in £50,000 in return for 53% and Francis would be MD.

We made it clear we needed a house on the island. We were shown a plot on a hill above the village of Mahau. Our next-door neighbours would be Philip and Gilda Nassief who had a lovely house above his Belfast Distillery. We designed the house on a piece of paper. It would consist of a central block/room for living with a dining area and a kitchen behind. On either side was a block consisting of two bedrooms with a bathroom in between. It was very simple and cheap to build. There would be a swimming pool behind and we had great views up and down the coast.

No time was wasted and the house was ready for us to visit in February 1967 although the pool was not finished.

Francis got a huge move on everybody and tidied up all the shops and the factory. He also started a construction business and got a contract to build a new police station, some houses, and later a hotel. He also added a franchise for Toyota to the division selling Bedford trucks and vans. Francis met up with a woman who was separated from a US soldier and who had a house in Roseau. He moved in and lived there.

For the first three or four years, everything went well. We made profits and we had marvellous virtually free holidays with friends to stay, including Jenny and Julian, Poppity's sister, Charlie and Mel Petre, David and Angela Darling, John and Flo Thomas and, of course, the wonderful John Ingledew – our partner. We'd buy our air tickets but we were then collected at the airport and had use of cars there. We usually kept quiet for the first week and thereafter, it would become rather social. We usually gave a party while there with food, drink, and a steel band. Lots of locals including the governor, a wonderfully pompous former civil servant in a white suit and a fly whisk, came to our parties.

A notable event was meeting Prince Charles at a party at Government House. He was an officer on a small minesweeper that was on the West India Station. He was clearly at a loose end the following day so we agreed to meet him at Castaways (more about this establishment later) in the morning. He duly arrived with Sergeant Officer, his detective, and we took him water skiing. He told us the news overnight that Richard Sharples, who I had sailed with in England, and who was the governor of the Bahamas, had been murdered. More amusingly Angela Darling was swimming when he arrived and tried very unsuccessfully to curtsy while up to her bottom in the sea.

He came back to our house and was a wonderfully grateful guest. We got a three-page handwritten thank you letter. Looking back, I think he was probably at a low ebb as Camilla had announced she would marry Andrew Parker Bowles.

Castaways was owned by Bill Harris, a cockney plumber, who fancied the local ladies. His sort of manageress was a Miss Shillingford but was known by everyone as Miss Puss. She lived with Bill but he slept with every girl who worked for him. Every month, all his girls were taken in an open truck into the hospital in Roseau where they were carrying out a trial of a contraceptive injection. This was known as the 'Bill's meat wagon'.

Another character who briefly came into our lives was Victor, Marquis of Bristol, and the last person to be flogged for robbing a jeweller in the Mayfair Hotel. He was not in good order but had a small house near Castaways.

Earlier, however, we got to know John Archbold, who was the son of Rockefeller's partner in Standard Oil. He was old but we had some amusing times with him. He had a ludicrous friend, Marian Montgomery, of Montgomery Ward. She was usually drunk but we also met Alec Waugh there who was writing a book based in the Caribbean. John had quite a large estate, which was managed by Gabriel Cadenas, a Cuban who was married to Gisela whose father had been dictator of Cuba before the war. They could not return but when John Archbold sold up as he was getting too old, they went to Puerto Rico. One year, Pops and I went to stay with them there.

Some other characters were Pete and Margie Brand, Americans, who had a hotel up the mountain in the rain forest. We were probably rather naïve but never got involved in drugs and sex parties, which were alleged to have gone on. After a few years, there were terrible storms and the hotel was badly damaged. Pete and Margie left, which was a pity because they had good parties.

Another interesting couple, who were obvious lesbians, ran a sandwich shop in Roseau. They were rather grand ladies and had a connection with the Tranby Croft affair. This was when one of the players took the rap for Edward VII cheating at cards. He retired to Dominica and obscurity.

A very colourful character was the vet, Brian Blatcher, who was married to a very pretty local girl who had been Miss Dominica. They had children who went to school in England. He built a splendid house and he clearly was very prosperous but there was not a huge amount of money being a vet in Dominica. He also had a farm over the other side of the island, which was pretty inaccessible up a long track. In Roseau, he had a small import/export business mainly exporting green coconuts in bags. We realised his secret a bit before the police, at which stage he fled the island and escaped capture. Of course, as a vet, he had a good knowledge of chemistry. He was growing quantities of marijuana on his farm, which he was processing there before inserting it into green coconuts that he exported.

Dominica was basically a Roman Catholic island and the Bishop was a Belgian. As an illustration of how society worked there, only the legitimate children of married parents inherited land or other assets. It was very common for even the most respectable men to have a number of what they called Outchildren, i.e., illegitimate, from different ladies. The children take the father's name, he recognises them, and pays their mothers some maintenance. Only if you have land or money do you get married.

The bishop told this story of a lovely lady who came to church regularly and helped clean it. She went to him and said, 'Bishop, will you please have a word with my daughter? She wants to get married. I was never married, none of my family were married, and it will cost a lot of money, which I don't have for a wedding. Please, Bishop, will you talk to her and make her give up this silly idea?'

The Bishop said he had no answer!

Another character was Bill White, alias Colonel White, commandant of Eaton Hall Officer Cadet School. He had retired and bought a small farm on the island. His wife hated it there but he was the life and soul of every party and there were many. Over the years we were there, from 1967 to 1976, we saw him gradually decline. He got robbed by the locals as he knew nothing about farming, started to run out of money, and took to the bottle. It was tragic but all too common. Eventually, his wife dragged him back to England and he died a few years later.

We always had a boat. First of all, I shipped the tin boat that I had in St Tropez and Elba and which I used to tow. We then bought a nice plastic waterski boat in Kensington High Street and shipped that out to Dominica. Then we decided we wanted something in which we could go to other islands. We bought a small cabin cruiser about 30 ft from a fellow member of the RYS and shipped that out.

John, Anna, John's new wife, Pops and I took it to Martinique. The seas are big between the islands and it was a very uncomfortable journey there and back. As we were returning and were off Dominica, the steering suddenly locked and we started going round in circles. The whole steering system had seized. Luckily, we were quite close to Castaways but had that happened on the passage from Martinique, we would have been in grave peril on the sea.

This boat continued to give problems and as we left to go home on one of our later trips, I said to Francis, 'I wish the bloody boat would sink.' A week later, we got a message from Francis saying he sadly had to tell us there had been a storm and our boat had sunk. How or why was not established but the insurers were satisfied and they paid up.

One rather unfortunate thing happened in about 1971. We were bringing the waterski boat ashore with Francis helping. It was hit by a wave he had not seen, knocked him down, and injured his back badly. He was never really the same again, having been Mr Fitness himself.

There were a number of setbacks to the business. Over two consecutive years, we had a huge crop of grapefruit that we were unable to sell as in the first year, the gassing plant that preserved the fruit was on strike. The following year, the government forgot to order any boxes so, again no sales of fruit. They had to be picked and thrown on the ground.

Then, in 1972, we were approached by Mark Gilbey who we had met in London. He was gay, lived in Tangier, and was a member of the Gilbey Gin family. He had a business part-owned by Heineken running distilleries in Africa. Mark became a good friend who we saw quite a bit of in London.

He suggested we build a distillery in Dominica on a 50:50 basis. It looked like a good opportunity as the government said we could have

preferential rates of duty for locally distilled products. I had long negotiations with a very slippery individual who was attorney general.

Mark felt it would be nice if he had a house on the island and so he
brought his great friend Oliver Messel, a connection of Poppity's,
together with his boyfriend the Great Dane to have a look at sites, etc.
Nothing came of it but the distillery was built and went into production of rum. The manager, Ken Robinson, had worked for Mark in
Sierra Leone.

An immediate problem was sugar cane does not grow in Dominica.
Francis organised for some to be grown but the price we had to pay
was four times what would have been the case in Barbados.

We also produced gin, Queen Elisabeth Gin, vodka that was just
cane spirit from Caroni in Trinidad, and whisky, Glen Mark. These
were brands owned by Mark's business, which supplied the essence
that was added to the cane spirit. There was nothing wrong with the
products as such but the government said it was too difficult to apply
lower rates of duty to our products. It was very difficult to sell Queen
Elisabeth Gin against Gordon's without a price differential. Ken
Robinson did his best and was up to all sorts of tricks with glycerine.
One of his great cries was, 'Not a drop is sold until it is 10 minutes old!'

We had borrowed the money from the bank for our stake in the
distillery and this remained a continuing problem as the venture was
loss-making.

Around 1971, I met up in London with Konrad Legge with my Wm
Brandts hat on. He was a controversial entrepreneur who was widely
regarded as an asset stripper. He understood I had West Indian
connections and he was interested in the Demerara company, quoted
in London, and with quite a bit of cash in hand. After Booker Brothers, it was the largest trading company in Guyana with substantial
interests in sugar – with a sugar mill and plantations.

I contacted the management in Guyana and they were very happy
to show me around and so I flew down to Georgetown via Trinidad for
a visit. It was very interesting and I made friends with the couple who

were running Guyana, Janet and Cheddi Jagan. They were regarded as dangerous communists by the UK and US governments but I found them charming and they invited me to dinner. Most interesting.

The population of Guyana is half African and half Indian and the elections went from one to the other. The Indians were in charge at this time as the Africans had made a mess of things. Anyhow, I returned to London, produced my report for Konrad, and got paid handsomely (fee to Wm Brandts). A week later Konrad put in a hostile offer for the Demerara company, which was ultimately successful. More fees for Brandts!

Despite work at Brandts until 1973 and then Mackenzie Hill in 1974-1975, we managed to do three weeks each year in Dominica. By 1975, things were becoming quite difficult there. There was a change of government and a new premier, Miss Eugenia Charles, who did not like us or Francis.

Francis had employed Tommy Coulthard, a lovely man and a long-time resident of the island as his assistant and a director but he was troubled by his back. In 1976, the government employed an English tax man seconded from the Inland Revenue here. Francis had played fast and loose with the local tax man and paid very little. They gave him a massive tax bill, which he thought better of and he got on the first flight to Miami.

We had come out in February and brought my mother and brother for their first visit. That was our last holiday in Dominica. John and I went out after Francis had done his runner to see whether we could get a work permit to employ a replacement. We were told we must employ a local man, which would have been hopeless.

John and I had a debenture over the assets of the company so we foreclosed under that with the agreement of the bank. We asked our auditors, Coopers and Lybrand in Trinidad to take over the administration of the business. They did this most efficiently for the next three years by closing unprofitable shops and the construction business as well as selling some properties.

The whole economy had been badly hit by the huge rise in oil prices and the recession in the mid-seventies. A small terrorist movement started and one of our good friends Ted Honeychurch, a white West Indian with an English wife and a farmer was murdered.

In October 1979, Hurricane Allen hit Dominica and did a huge amount of damage. The distillery was completely destroyed as was the lime/cocoa/copra factory.

We were well-insured and so Coopers put in the claim which was settled so that we could repay the bank and the creditors. We entered into negotiations to sell the business to the Coopers man running it, Julius Timothy, who was actually a Dominican. This went on for at least two years but, eventually, John, Anna, Pops, and I went back to Dominica in early 1982 whereby we sold the business for much less than we paid and on a phased basis.

At least we retrieved something. It was not a successful business investment but I regret not one little bit as it was a magical experience and we had so much fun. My only sadness was we never got any of our children there. Initially, they were too young and then we always went during school time.

WM BRANDT'S SONS & CO

*A*fter completion of the sale of Burkes in 1967, I went back to WI Carr and picked up with my old clients. I quickly decided it was not what I wanted to do long term. I had a number of outside interests. I was a director of Great American Industries and owned a few shares. I owned about 40% of Casa Pupo and was a director. I was chairman of Welland Textiles in Market Harborough where I had a significant shareholding. I was also buying my 26% interest in AC Shillingford in Dominica.

David Stapleton went to visit his brother, Michael, in Hong Kong where he met a number of Chinese investors. They were keen to speculate on the London Stock Exchange and David had agreed to open dealing accounts for them. This was an extension of the business where we had opened dealing accounts for a small number of investment managers. I suppose we were facilitating their insider dealing, but it certainly helped bring in the business.

One of David's new clients became a well-known billionaire some years later. We used to discuss what to buy and when to sell, and by and large, made money. This was the beginning of David's hugely successful business in the Far East after I left.

Then, a man called Michael Graham Jones telephoned out of the blue and asked me to lunch with him. He was in effect a head hunter. He said Wm Brandts, a small family-controlled merchant bank but two-thirds owned by National and Grindlays Bank were looking to expand their corporate side and was I interested. It was a board appointment and so I said, 'Yes.'

The next step was to meet the senior directors. I went round to 30 Fenchurch Street a few days later where I was shown into a room with four large desks behind which were two elderly Brandts. Walter was the chairman and there was also the much younger Peter Brandt. There was also an outsider, Frank Welsh. They offered me the job to head up the corporate finance department. I would get a salary of about £17,000 and bonuses as well as share options. This was perfect.

Initially, I was not appointed a director but was on the writing paper with another very senior employee termed as advisers to the board. About a week later, they discovered I was not a chartered accountant nor did I have any legal qualifications. The individual who was in charge of the department and who I would have been over the top of was a chartered accountant!

It was decided I would not run the corporate finance department but they had lots of things I could do. They provided me with an office and secretary, Olivia Clough Taylor. The office manager was an ex-brigadier of marines, Jack Wills. He told me to go to Harrods and buy suitable furniture. I bought a desk, round conference table, four dining chairs, and two upright upholstered leather chairs. Finally, I said I needed a calculating machine. I recollect this cost of £350 in 1967 and was only a few years later superseded by electronic machines. Indeed, I had one of the first made by a British company, Lamson Industries.

Brandts had a policy of investing in industrial businesses and Frank Welsh ran this side. They had bought a Sheffield special steel business, Dunford and Elliot. They told me they had put some money up for a friend of Peter Brandt, who was creating a big recording studio complex in Piccadilly. They had also bought into a company, HJ Mugdan, which franchised and equipped laundrettes.

I became a director of both companies to represent the bank's interest. Neither were sensible investments. One of the Mugdan directors turned out to be a crook and the business collapsed about a year later. The recording studio was in the wrong place, had no parking, and soundproofing problems. It eventually ran out of money and collapsed.

Brandt's had also invested in a quoted company Sound Diffusion based near Brighton. I joined their board of directors to represent the bank. They put sound and call systems into hospitals and commercial premises. It made excellent profits and the shares were rising when I realised they were capitalising the cost of every installation and not writing anything off. I insisted with the auditors that proper amortization must be carried out which dramatically reduced the profits. The two brothers who ran the business were furious and insisted I resign. Sadly the business collapsed a few years later but we had sold all the bank's shares by then.

They then realised I had a paid-for trip on a bi-monthly basis to New York. They had a representative office with an older retired American banker, Bill Bogdan.

Brandts were not very clever really. They had had to sell out to National and Grindlays when they were nearly insolvent following having made loans secured on Salad Oil which turned out not to exist. They had subsequently lent money secured on gaming machines owned by an outfit in Las Vegas. Bogdan and lawyers had done a good job and following default by the borrower had established ownership of the machines, about $1.5 million.

I was sent to New York to meet up with Bogdan and the lawyers and sell the gaming machines. Two companies had expressed an interest. I met with the first who were only interested at a very low valuation. The second interested party was a Mr Robert Vesco. He was not a nice man but we got on quite well, and I joined him for dinner in his huge suite at the Regency Hotel. We did a deal and the following day his lawyers put $1.5 million in escrow, which got all the bank's money back.

A number of years later, Vesco became notorious as the most wanted man by the FBI when he stole all the money and investments of IOS, Bernie Cornfeld's company, having moved in as a white knight to save the business. He went to Costa Rica with over $ 130 million and was never extradited.

At about this time Robert Maxwell had tried to sell his company Pergamon Press to Reliant Industries of the USA. It was discovered the accounts were fraudulent and he was removed from running the business, which was a mandate given to Brandts. I attended a meeting where Maxwell was present and shouting the odds. At one stage, it was suggested I should take on the task of running Pergamon but it was decided a more senior director, Alastair Thompson, who was a bit older should do it. It was a ghastly job and a real poisoned chalice, and so I was very lucky I dodged that one.

A very interesting project I took on was to be a director of Aeriel. This was a company set up by all the leading merchant banks to develop a computerised platform for dealing in stocks and shares. They were fed up with the stock-exchange monopoly on buying and selling charging high, fixed commission rates. It was funded by the merchant banks and I was asked to be a director as I had been a stockbroker.

Over about two years, the company developed a workable platform that would easily deal in fixed-interest stocks and bonds. Two things then happened. The Bank of England became frightened they could lose control of the market in government securities and the stockbrokers became very scared. The stockbrokers agreed to dramatically cut their rates of commission and the Bank of England forbade us from dealing in government stocks. Aeriel was shelved but we had delivered something that was nearly twenty years ahead of its time.

I was then asked to advise the board of Bradleys of York, a substantial quoted house builder where the chairman, Mr Bradley, had used the company's workers on his personal property and borrowed money from the company, which was in trouble. We got him to repay some of the money and did a deeply discounted rights issue. It was good practice for later encounters at Lloyd's but I had a very rowdy and angry meeting of shareholders to explain why we were not prosecuting Mr Bradley and why the rights issue was priced as it was. In the end, all was agreed.

One day, I got a call from the front desk in the banking hall. They knew I was a sailing man and referred an individual up to me who had come in and asked to borrow money. This was John Fairfax, the first man to row singlehanded across the Atlantic. He had been brought up in the Argentine and worked as a pearl diver in the Pacific. He was short and stocky and clearly very strong. He told me he had been in the water, cleaning barnacles off the bottom of his boat with a knife when a shark attacked him. He dived under the shark and cut its belly open with his knife killing the shark.

He wanted money to firstly make a film of him fighting a shark with only a knife, flippers, and a mask. He then wanted to row the Pacific, which had not been done before. I said Brandts would not be interested but my colleagues at Great American Industries might be. So, he accompanied me the next time I went to America.

GAI were interested and chartered a boat in the Bahamas with a cameraman. They chucked some meat over the stern and John Fairfax jumped in and attacked a shark. Despite getting a nasty bite on the arm, he killed the shark which was at least 12-ft long. Unfortunately, the film made was of very poor quality. You could more or less see him killing the shark but it was not of a quality to sell to television, which had been the objective. GAI then helped him put together sponsorship for a row across the Pacific.

We returned to England and John became a frequent visitor to our house in Pembroke Road. One day he brought a girlfriend, Sylvia, who looked pretty tough and who he had chosen to join him on the row across the Pacific. In due course, he returned to the USA and John Thomas went to San Francisco with him where plans were finalised for the Pacific row. Twice they started under the Golden Gate Bridge but a change of tide sent them back. On each occasion, John and Sylvia had clearly smoked a few joints and were just giggling. Eventually, they went a bit further down the coast and they got away and disappeared for many months. No GPS or satellite phones in those days. About a year later they turned up in Queensland.

John then appeared again in London. On the row, they had gone to Washington Island miles from anywhere in the middle of the Pacific where he had found a ship that was beached and abandoned and was full of lead. He wanted finance to go and retrieve the lead. I said not possible and with that, he disappeared out of my life, although I heard tell of him from time to time.

One day I received a call from Lord Aldington, chairman of National and Grindlays, to go and see him. He had heard I had driven the length of Africa and had a job for me in Kenya. The government sugar industry in Western Kenya at Chemelil was in a financial mess. It was financed by the Germans, the British Crown Agents and Shell, banked with National and Grindlays and was run by Booker Brothers. I was to go to Kenya, report to Bruce Mackenzie the Minister of Agriculture and organise a refinancing.

Over a twelve-month period, I put together a refinancing that involved getting a lot more money out of the German development people in Dusseldorf, and some out of Shell and the Crown Agents. In doing this, I visited Kenya about ten times and Dusseldorf at least twice.

The National and Grindlays people in Nairobi were hugely helpful, charming, and very hospitable. They lived in great style with indoor and outdoor servants, chauffeurs, and were big fishes in a small pond. No wonder none of them wanted promotion on return home!

I also saw a lot of George Moody Stuart who was the Booker manager at Chemelil. They were working on a new project to grow sugar with a factory not too far away at Mumias. Later, I helped them get some finance for this from the Germans. My main recommendation was that they had to increase the price of sugar in the domestic market where they were selling at a loss.

We put the finances back on an even keel but they failed to change the policy so they got back into trouble but after I had left Grindlays. That was Africa then. One of the nice things was I could change my first-class ticket for two ordinary tickets and Pops and I had at least two lovely trips and holidays in Kenya.

On one of my trips to New York, I had met a Texan oil man, Fred Chambers, who had a company called C&K Petroleum. He turned up in London and said he would like me as Wm Brandts to put together a syndicate to bid for exploration blocks in the North Sea. He had signed up Kerr Magee as the operator; they were one of the premier oil-exploration companies in the world and based in Oklahoma. I persuaded the Rank Organisation and Chase Investment Corp in New York to invest. We had to show the government we had enough funds to drill wells if we were allocated blocks. This was the first round of the sale of blocks in the North Sea for exploration. If we were allocated any blocks in which Kerr Magee were interested and they had the last word, it was agreed I would be MD of the company.

Fred Chambers became a good friend and we had a lot of fun together. One of his directors was George Bush senior who was then the US spokesperson at the UN. We saw a bit of him in New York and at one famous dinner, Poppity discovered his nickname among close friends was poppy so they got on famously.

Sadly, we were not offered the only three blocks Kerr Magee were interested in but we were offered what turned out to be Brent, one of the most productive of all oil fields in the North Sea. Kerr Magee did not fancy it. We dissolved the syndicate with much sadness. I might have been an oil man!

It did, however, lead me to get a call from Morgan Grenfell who offered me a job running their oil investment side, which they were establishing. It was not a main board appointment and so I turned it down. I had also earlier turned down the opportunity of going to run a new office in Australia.

Flights to the USA could always be interesting. I used to travel first class on Pan American on a 6.30 pm flight. I would do a day's work in the office and get to Heathrow at 5.30 pm. At about 8 o'clock the stewardess would come to say dinner was served. I'd leave my comfortable seat and be shown to a table for four people. I'd then be introduced to the other two or three people there. There was a pot of caviar or smoked salmon, then a piece of rare beef was carved at the table, followed by a pudding of some sort, all washed down with decent wine.

On one such trip, I sat next to a charming older man who turned out to be a Goulandris and chairman of the Greek Line. He did not know Brandts but knew we did a lot of ship finance. I introduced our ship-finance people to him and I believe we financed at least four or five ships for him over the next few years. It was well-worth travelling first class.

My next project was an approach from Peter Learmonth, a retired naval officer, who ran a successful scrap-metal business. He wanted to build a mini steel mill processing scrap rather than ore on a site at Sheerness. This would be a first in the UK. He became a friend but was an exceptionally difficult person to deal with.

We got a prospectus together with WI Carr as brokers and got quite a bit of interest but not enough to proceed. I reluctantly told him he needed to get a company involved who had built and operated similar steel mills. He found just such a company in Canada who came on board as partners and shareholders. Unfortunately, they wanted Kleinwort's to be the lead bankers to the issue with Brandts in a slightly secondary role.

I worked with George Pinto and his assistant David Clementi who later became deputy governor of the Bank of England and chairman of the BBC. The issue and the company were a great success and Learmonth made a great deal of money. I had nursed his idea for a long time and correctly advised him how to get it off the ground but I never, even when I used to see him socially, did I ever get a word of thanks from him.

Some years previously, Martin Mays Smith had joined as banking director, which was a great bonus as he was very experienced, having been at the Bank of England and Barclays. We worked very closely together.

One day, an old fifties and sixties property man, Bernard Myers who'd had a few problems a few years previously, came into the office and saw Martin and me. He had two properties ripe for development with remarkable planning consents as to density and use. One was an office block on a car park in the middle of Birmingham and the other was a large old building in Princes Street, Edinburgh where he had a pre-let. Birmingham was easy to let and so we agreed to put up 100% of the money on a formula that gave us a shareholding in the company depending on the success of the development after we had been repaid.

Bernard Myers was helped by his son Martin who was a junior partner at Jones Lang and by a clever young man, David Olivestone. Both of them later had great success with large listed property companies but Martin Myers was unlucky and I believe he got caught in the 2007 or one of the earlier downturns.

I became a director of a company called Site Projections, which had offices in Berkeley Square. Before we knew where we were, Bernard Myers was buying more sites and financing them with institutions. He had an uncanny ability to get around the planners. Birmingham and Edinburgh were both successful developments and we got our money back and a shareholding in Site Projections. Sadly, after I left Brandts and during the secondary banking crisis in 1974, Site Projections became insolvent.

Another interesting project was Russ Hill Hotel, whose representatives came to see me to raise the money to build on to their existing hotel near Gatwick Airport. Secured by a first charge on the existing hotel, I lent them 100% finance to build about fifty rooms and a huge dining room to cater for delayed flights at Gatwick. All was built within budget and the resultant operation was hugely profitable. I did not take an equity stake but required them to refinance by way of a mortgage and repay us together with a fee of around £100,000. This proved to be one of the most profitable deals I did for the bank.

We had started to become quite well-known as property financiers. We were hoping to get a mandate to float a private property company of some size and, to get the issue going, we asked the three senior directors to lunch. I had been away in the USA and Martin Mays Smith forgot to tell the dining room that our guests were very orthodox Jews. Imagine my horror when hot ham was produced for lunch. Our guests were not pleased, and we never did do the issue.

My final significant project was to build a chipboard mill at Stirling in Scotland. Behind the project was Till Hill, the timber people based near Farnham. I put together a prospectus to raise the money to build the mill under the name, Scottish Timber Products. The supply of the necessary timber was agreed with the Lonsdale estates and the Scottish Forestry Commission. Scottish institutions and the Bank of Scotland were keen to invest as were my friends from Chase International Investment Corporation. Success with Sheerness Steel helped. The objective was to put shredded timber in one end and sheets of chipboard at the other, for which there would be a ready market.

We built in a very large contingency to cope with unforeseen events. I left Brandts just as we completed the fundraising and the factory was being built. Sadly, my successors allowed the contingency to be spent on downstream activities such as bonding, cutting, etc. This was supposed to improve margins. Unfortunately, the secondary banking crisis had a dire effect on the building industry and sales dived. With no contingency, the company went into receivership and then liquidation. It was a great idea that never got going again.

In 1970, my friend John Millard Barnes who was the senior surveyor at the Church Commissioners rang me and said he was sending round to me a young property man. He had a development the church would like to be involved in but they could not deal with a private company controlled by one man. If I could interject Brandts between the development and the church so they were dealing with Brandts, that would work. This was Charles Mackenzie Hill with whom we subsequently did a lot of business at Brandts and who I was then asked to become their finance director. All that merits a separate chapter.

In any case, Brandts had got into a real mess in 1972. With no reference to the Brandts credit committee, Peter Brandt and Toby Aldington agreed to lend £3.5 million (Brandts' capital was £3 million) to an Argentinian who was buying Harrods BA, a company quoted in London. There was quite a lot of cash and he was meant to own a huge store, other shops, and a lot of property in Buenos Aires.

He turned out to be a crook and openly stole the £3.5 million so, Brandts were effectively insolvent. It was agreed the Brandt family would sell their remaining one-third to National and Grindlays and Citibank would take an interest in Grindlays and help manage Brandts.

The best asset was the building in Fenchurch Street. Brandts had a seventy-year lease from an insurance company who in turn had a lease from a property company with the freehold owned by the Mercers Company. I was asked to obtain a valuation. I included in the instructions to assume the whole of the benefit of the merger of the senior interests to Brandts should accrue in the valuation to Brandts. I was told this inflated the valuation by nearly £1 million but nobody queried this and the Brandt family benefited.

Some two years previously, I had proposed we beef up our corporate side by recruiting someone I knew, Michael Andrews, who had been at Hill Samuel and Samuel Montagu and had a good reputation as a corporate finance man. My colleagues turned the idea down because he was too much of a heavyweight. Now Grindlays and Citibank hired Michael Andrews as chief executive. There was a mass walkout at Brandts led by Peter Brandt. His father retired and nearly all the senior people went to a small outfit, Edward Bates. I had come across them and decided I did not like the three individuals who everyone would be joining. Peter Brandt promised me the deputy MD position if I would come but I decided to stay.

Martin Mays Smith also declined and went to Kleinwort's. Just before he left, Peter Brandt took me to lunch and apologised that they had never done anything about share options and thanked me for all the money I had made for the bank. He then handed me an envelope. I opened it later and it contained a cheque for £15,000 from the Brandt family.

Sadly, two years later at the height of the secondary banking crisis, Bates went bust and all those who had bought shares to capitalise the business lost everything.

Andrews brought in some good people but it was not a happy ship. He was volatile and if you wanted a decision or approval of something it was necessary to ask his secretary whether he was in a good mood or not. If he was not, forget about anything until he was. He also shouted at people and reduced some directors to tears. He was a first-class corporate finance man but a very bad chief executive.

After a year of this, I decide the bank had become totally risk-averse. I had been there five years of which the first four were wonderful. I was more or less allowed to do my own thing and work pretty independently. I know I made a great deal of money for the bank but it was time to move on.

MACKENZIE HILL

*I*started to look around and was approached by Paul Shewell, a very senior partner of Price Waterhouse. He told me he was the auditor of a very big property company. They desperately needed a finance director who could raise money and stand up to the executive chairman who was the driving force. The package was a salary of £40,000, a car, a chauffeur and all the usual benefits. I had to say yes before the company was revealed. I did so and found my next employment was with Charles Mackenzie Hill who was well-known to me

Charles was educated at Stowe and then Cambridge where he had a reputation as a very fine rugby player and an outstanding boxer. He was unbeaten as an amateur until he fought Billy Walker, who briefly became heavyweight champion of Great Britain a few years later, but not before Charles knocked him down.

I was introduced to him in 1970 when he had already built up a considerable property development business in the UK and was starting in Europe. He was building warehouses near Luton and, with a French-speaking friend, Robin Crowther, had seen the opportunity for warehousing adjacent to the Charles de Gaulle airport, which was being built.

My introduction came via John Millard Barnes, an old friend, who was the chief surveyor at the Church Commissioners. He sent Charles to see me as he was keen to buy a development Charles was doing but felt he could not be seen to be dealing with such a small company. He suggested we put Brandts in between the church and Mackenzie Hill. This made sense and we made a good turn out of the deal.

I financed a number of developments for him, which involved buying the site, getting planning, building, letting to a tenant, and selling to an institution. We provided finance with a share of the equity. Our best deal was a site for 200 houses adjacent to Newport Pagnell Services on the M1. We put up 100% finance for half the profit. In the event, we made around £250,000 on an outlay of around £1 million.

About a year later, Hambros asked him to advise on redeveloping the waterfront warehouses in Hong Kong, owned by the Swire Group. He put the deal together with their help and finished up with a 20% shareholding in what became Swire Properties. I then had to compete with Hambros for his business. The company's offices were in Grosvenor Gardens. The accounting function was competently run and my job was really financial policy and raising money for the group's programme of developments as well as saying no to Charles.

By this time there were operations in Paris and Lyon; redeveloping the centre of St Etienne, Stuttgart in Germany with a massive office development; an office in Madrid run by an Anglo Spaniard, John Gomez Hall; a small office in Amsterdam; and then an office in Sao Paulo and Rio de Janeiro and in Phoenix Arizona. This was in addition to a number of offices throughout the UK.

With hindsight, it was a crazy setup. There was no substance to the group. Charles rushed around finding sites and he and I and the local people found the finance. What we did have was competent management in these offices, capable of letting out and supervising building contracts. Charles had huge magnetism and persuaded very good people to come and work for him. The overheads of the group were considerable and it was always necessary to sell completed developments. When I joined, we had three aeroplanes, including a Cessna Citation executive jet and a helicopter. This involved employing a number of pilots. Once a month, I used to do Paris, Stuttgart, and Madrid and, in theory, the planes made sense. What I found though was that the pilots too often had run out of hours just when we needed to fly.

My main sources of finance, other than institutional investors, was the Bank of Chicago in London and an Arab French Bank in Paris, BAII.

I went to Barcelona with Charles on one occasion together with John Gomez Hall where we bought a hotel on Las Ramblas. It was old fashioned and a bit run down but was a good site for offices. In the event, we sold the pictures on the walls for more than we paid for the whole building and contents.

I also went twice to Sao Paulo and Rio where Charles through friendship on the polo field had a contact with the Vestey family. They had a lot of money stuck in Brazil, which they could not get out. I put a deal together with Vesteys and Shell whereby we built high-rise office buildings in Sao Paulo and Rio for Shell to occupy, financed in part by Vesteys and Shell themselves. We did the project management and made good fees, which paid for our people and our offices.

Charles lived in considerable style at Cosgrove Hall near Milton Keynes. He had parted from his wife and had three sons. He told me he was going to see Millfield for them. I said, 'For goodness sake, go in an office car and certainly not the helicopter with Mackenzie Hill plastered all over it.'

Anyhow, he got delayed and took the helicopter. The following day, he was very upset when he told me Millfield were delighted to take all three of his sons on the basis they charged according to parents means. They said they would look to him to provide two bursaries for each son. He would, in due course, be paying nine school fees!

Towards the middle of 1974, the secondary banking crisis had taken hold and it was getting more and more difficult to finance the purchase of sites and developments. The final straw was Charles finding a wonderful site in Brussels ripe for development. He committed to buying it but all my efforts to raise finance failed. Somehow, we got out of the deal.

Up until Christmas, I was rushing all over Europe sorting out problems. For Christmas, we were at North Breache with my mother and the three children. On Christmas Eve, I felt pretty ill but thought nothing of it and went out with a gun and shot some rabbits and a pheasant. That night, we went to church and then the children were wildly excited on Christmas morning. I smoked a cigarette and had a glass of champagne at lunchtime but felt awful and so I retired to bed with a cough, feeling ghastly.

Our local doctor came to see me and said I had a bit of bronchitis but not to worry. Over the next few days, I got worse and then our wonderful London doctor, Johnny Norcliffe Roberts was called by Poppity. He said it sounded as if I had pneumonia. To cut a long story short, I was taken on a stretcher in an ambulance to Mount Alvernia in Guildford where they confirmed I had double pneumonia and was very ill. I was there for ten days. A very large nun used to turn me over, head down, and pummel my back.

I never had a temperature and never totally lost my appetite, so my mother used to bring me nice things to eat, as the food was not good. When I got home to North Breache, I was pretty weak but I had not had a cigarette for nearly three weeks and so I swore I would give up. This I did, and I never smoked again. It was tough, to begin with as I was quite a heavy smoker and the stress of my job had not helped in that direction.

At the end of January, I went back to work only to find things had not improved. The Mackenzie Hill Group was very short of cash. Just before Christmas, Christopher Bland, later chairman of BBC, BT, and lots of things, had come to the office and suggested Charles should buy Oddbins from the receiver. He was working for a fringe bank who were significant creditors and was a director. I said to Charles it was a distraction and anyhow there was no money and he should not get involved. His great friend Charles Lousada also looked at it and decided against.

Anyhow, on my return in January, I discovered Charles had bought the business for £1 and had given 30% to Nicholas Baile and John Ing who had been running the Peter Dominic chain of off-licences and so he had management. Unfortunately, the business consisted of twelve shops on leases in poor locations with about four exceptions, about £800,000 of stock, mainly wine and £1 million of debt. The company was therefore insolvent on day one.

I then told Charles he could no longer afford to employ me. He was not going to do any new business, the situation was pretty grim, and he would have to spend much of his time sorting out problems and getting in as much cash as possible. He accepted I should leave but then said would I look after Oddbins for him. I said I had advised against but, yes, if he gave me 20% of his shares. He bridled at that and we agreed I got an 8% shareholding in the company.

Before going on the board, I went to see Sir Kenneth Cork, who was the leading insolvency practitioner of the day to ask whether I was putting myself in a dangerous position by being a director of an insolvent company. Christopher Bland had resigned as soon as he could. Cork said to me, 'If you can see a way of paying your way and light at the end of the tunnel then you have no worries.'

I joined the board and we found a way forward. We were able to buy spirits like Bells Whisky and Beefeater Gin on sixty-days credit. By taking no margin and selling at cost, we could turn it into cash in about ten days. This gave us considerable cash as a result of which we were able to open new shops and had plenty of working capital. Baile and Ing were good on the wine side and made good margins there. Oddbins became a bit of a cult business with a great selection of New World wines from Australia, New Zealand, Chile and the USA.

About a year later, we were approached by our competitor Bottoms Up who were owned by a flamboyant Spanish entrepreneur, Ruis Mateos. He was very rich and successful but had a somewhat dubious reputation. I was deputed by the board to go and see what he had to say in Barcelona. I had a busy day and so I took a late flight, intending to go straight to my hotel and then meet Ruiz Mateos in the morning.

I ate dinner on the plane but was surprised to find a car had been sent for me. I was driven to a large skyscraper and ushered up to the top floor where it was clear I was expected for dinner although it was now at least 11 pm.

After drinks, we sat down to dinner, which went on until about 2 am. At this stage, my host said, 'Right, now let's get down to business.' I am afraid I absolutely refused to talk business, which rather upset Mr Mateos. I went back to my hotel and met again in the morning. We did not really agree on anything and so I returned and reported no deal.

About two years later, Bottoms Up went bust and Ruiz Mateos' empire collapsed around him. He was arrested for fraud. Meanwhile, Oddbins prospered.

In 1975, receivers had foreclosed on Nassauer Bros and the London Wine Company. They were in the business of buying wine for investment for a large number of investors. Unfortunately, they failed to label the wine in their warehouse as being the property of each investor and so the receiver seized all of it. Christie's had an auction to sell it all. John Ing and I went to the auction. John told me what to buy and I did the bidding. We bought about 35% of what was available. I also bought about 500 bottles of 1963 and 1966 port for myself at about £3 per bottle. Of course, I should have bought first and second-growth clarets but I still have some of the '63 and '66 left as I write this in 2019

Charles was also a director and was keen to realise his investment. So, in 1979, we successfully sold the company to Seagrams for about £6 million. Nick Baile had done a wonderful job and there were seventy Oddbins shops in the UK and five in Paris. The turnover was around £75 million but the profits were only around £200,000. However, Nick had started to get distracted by trying to put together an encyclopaedia of wine. We had all made quite a lot of money.

Charles was a shadow of his former self. He had successfully kept the property company afloat but had to sell the valuable interest in Swire Properties and was left with very little. Cosgrove had gone as well. What he should have done was put the company into liquidation in 1974 like others did and then start again with a clean sheet. It says a lot for his tenacity that he kept on fighting and his creditors undoubtedly benefited.

Charles and I continued as friends and met up regularly. In the early 1980s, he came up with a proposition to buy from the chairman, who had retired to Jersey, a 27% stake in James Wilkes, a quoted company. This would give us control.

I was a director of Alva Investment Trust, ADD run by my friend Jacques Delacave It was managed by Throgmorton Fund Managers who owned 29% with various clients. , I went to see Bob Segrove, the chief executive who was happy we were going to do something with the company. I got a verbal undertaking he would always give me first refusal if he sold the shareholding.

I put together a small syndicate, which included my friend Michael Davies who was a director of a number of large companies and had run Imperial Foods. I became executive chairman and we terminated the existing managing director. Wilkes owned Joseph Quarnby in Huddersfield, the largest manufacturer of beer mats in Europe, Deritend Engineering in Birmingham, which made huge machines which made and printed packaging like Cornflakes packets, and three small printing companies also in Birmingham, which were loss-making.

There were good people running Quarnby and Deritend but they were paid very badly. I put their remuneration up which seemed to galvanise the performance of both companies. I closed down the printing companies and sold the machines as there was no buyer for the companies.

Charles was on the board but had only a token shareholding. He came up with the idea of buying a landfill business operating three sites, two in Barrow in Furness and one in Sheffield. We bought them for a tiny amount of cash and some shares. It was a very profitable business. Everything was going well when I received a call from Stephen Hinchcliffe who told me he had bought a 29% interest from Throgmorton. I called Segrove who said he had had a good offer and so he sold.

He had behaved like a complete shit but I said I would see whether I could work with Hinchcliffe, who was Sheffield-based. However, it was soon clear that would be difficult as he wished to be the chief executive. He was a flash individual with a helicopter that would be run on the company. He also had a brassey blond wife and a powder-blue Rolls Royce. His way of doing business was not mine but he had a following and the shares went up. I decided to resign provided Hinchcliffe arranged for any member of my syndicate's shares to be placed. This was done and most of us sold at a good profit to our cost. Some two years later, Hinchcliffe was accused of fraud and was sentenced to three years in prison.

By this time Charles was not at all well and had cancer. He came to stay at North Breache, drank a bottle of whisky on Friday night, ate nothing, and came out shooting all day on Saturday. At the last drive of the day, he shot two pheasants with a single shot, about which he was very excited. He drank another bottle of whisky that night, ate virtually nothing, departed after lunch and was dead on Tuesday morning. He was a remarkable character but it was rather a case of how are the mighty fallen?

LIFE AT HOME

I now need to go back in time. While all these business activities were going on, there was plenty of action at home on the family and social front so, to go back.

Pembroke Road was a marvellous house and especially the garden and swimming pool. I'd had the latter put in in 1967 when Guinness had paid me compensation for loss of office when I'd had no contract. The double gates at the bottom of the garden into Logan Place made construction easy and we finished with a 30ft pool and a round children's paddling pool attached to it.

Amanda, William, and Rupert all learned to swim and it was much appreciated by their friends and at parties in the summer. In April 1966, after the wedding, we had the reception for Jenny, Pops' sister, and Julian Goldsmid in our house and garden.

A few years later, there was the reception for the old girlfriend, Bridget Holt, who I've already mentioned. Her first marriage had been to Ricky Hutton who was a Woolworth heir with far too much money who turned out to be gay. The second one, at Pembroke Road, was to another American and the heir to the Simoniz car-polish fortune. During the honeymoon, he disappeared. It had been a ruse for some trust fund money. After the disappointing news from Derek Clogg,

Bridget went off to America and we did not see her for some years. She was a very sad person.

Pops had lots of problems having children and was put to bed for a few months before each premature birth. The wonderful George Wynne Williams, gynaecologist, and even more wonderful Johnnie Norcliffe Roberts, our GP, made it all possible. With Will, I got a French lady in to do some cooking. She was a very good cook but Pops said she was very dirty. We used to have dinner in our bedroom at a table.

Amanda was two months premature and went down to less than 3 lbs but when she got home, she was a fine, fat baby but rather antisocial with other children. Will, who came two years later was not quite as premature but was a sickly child. He also did not speak until he was three years old. I insisted he went to a specialist to ensure he was not retarded. All was OK and when he did start to talk, he never stopped.

Nanny Lock, who was a Plymouth Brother, although she did not promote it, who would take Amanda to the seaside in Sandbanks, gave way to Nanny Hetherington who had been Pops' nanny but not before we employed a very professional Norland nanny in a starched uniform. The children hated her and Pops was in a terrible state. I came back from the office and told her to go. She was pretty difficult and refused until I said I would get the police to remove her. I had to give her money for a hotel for the night in addition to her pay for a few days.

We also had Nanny Eileen who was very Irish. She was tasked with getting sickly Will to eat and used to give him a spoonful of sherry to help. We then had a dustman's strike. I had an incinerator at the bottom of the garden where I used to burn the garden rubbish. With no bin collection, I burned the rubbish in my incinerator. I found a vast number of empty cans of Guinness at the bottom of the bags and we realised Eileen was a drinker. We'd had our suspicions because on a Saturday Morning if we pushed the pram up the Earls Court Road, the children used to say a Victoria Wine shop was Nanny's shop.

She got very difficult in the end and Pops had to get rid of her in Bembridge. Nanny Hetherington came to the rescue before we employed Sheila who stayed with us for a number of years. I did not really like her though as she was very possessive of the children.

In 1971, we went for our usual three weeks at our house in Dominica. On getting there, Pops suddenly started to feel sick especially in the morning. She thought she had flu but someone said are you sure you are not pregnant. She took a test and sure enough she was. While travelling she had forgotten to take one pill. That was enough! We had been told she should not try to have more children so on return, suggestions were made about terminations. We had no trouble in saying, no we would proceed.

In the event, it was another very difficult pregnancy. When Rupert was born by caesarean at about eight months in Queen Charlotte's, the doctors were worried about Pops and the baby. I waited in the room while dear Johnnie Norcliffe Roberts was present at the delivery. He came back up to the room and said Pops was OK but had lost a lot of blood but I should not expect the little boy to live.

Well, he did and after about three weeks we got Rupert home where he did well but his fingers were stuck together, sort of webbed. For sickness, Pops had taken a drug called Debendox which some years later we discovered had caused deformities in some children. When he was three, he had two horrible operations in a hospital in Kingston to separate his fingers, which involved skin grafts from his bottom. He was left with heavily scarred hands to this day.

Sheila was frightened of small babies and so we got a sweet New Zealand girl, Colleen, to look after Rupert. So, we had Sheila, Colleen and Lydia.

With Rupert on the way, we had decided to build on to Pembroke Road. We put two single rooms on a bit of flat roof on the second floor and we added a small conservatory to the end of the galley-like kitchen, which gave us a breakfast room.

We had a black Labrador Flynne who we used to let out of the front door onto Pembroke Road at 10.30 at night. He either went into the gardens of the flats next door or sometimes he went down

Pembroke Road, crossed Warwick Road and did his business in some waste ground there, which is now a massive Tesco supermarket. He'd return twenty minutes later.

About a year after Rupert was born, Sheila decided to move on and we replaced her with a younger girl called Hillary who stayed with us until we moved to North Breache in 1976.

A TRIP IN TIME TO THE RYS

I've already mentioned how my father's old colleague Reggie Macdonald-Buchanan proposed I join the RYS in 1962. I was duly elected in 1964 so at the time of writing this I am No 8 and quite often the senior member present so, I have just proposed the vote of thanks to the Commodore at the Spring Meeting of the membership which is now nearly 600 with naval members. I think it was about 290 when I was elected.

In about 1967, Michael Boyle asked me whether I would join him and Peter Vanneck in owning and sailing a Daring, a 35 ft day-sailing racing boat, requiring a crew of three, in Cowes. I readily agreed and in the summer, we used to spend roughly every third weekend in Cowes.

Peter was new in our lives – Group Captain, the Hon Sir Peter Vanneck. He had commanded motor torpedo boats and then transferred to the Fleet Air Arm during the war. Afterwards, he commanded the Royal Auxiliary Air Force and flew jets in Malta, which is why he was a Group Captain. He was a partner in Rowe and Pitman, a very leading firm of stockbrokers and a deputy chairman of the stock exchange.

Both he and Michael loved dressing up and they always went sailing in a white shirt, tie, and sailing coat with RYS buttons on it. In Cowes week, Peter organised the parties; he was also a flag officer and then commodore of the Royal London Yacht Club. We'd start with a party at the Royal London; then there would follow, on consecutive nights, the Squadron Ball, the London Ball, the Town Ball, fireworks evening, the Squadron Dinner, and it all finished with the Bembridge Ball by which time we were all basket cases as we had been sailing all day.

Peter had found a lovely young man, John Sichel, who was an impoverished medical student with a widowed mother living in Yarmouth. We paid his expenses and he came and did the foredeck, handling the spinnaker. I could do it when he was not available but he was rather better than me.

We were never very successful and it is fair to say that on a few occasions when none of us could make it John sailed the boat, Dauntless No 3 Daring, and did a bit better than us sailing with his girlfriend. She was also a medical student who he later married.

I rarely went to Cowes without Poppity who used to come sailing with us. We stayed in the RYS and had some good parties there. She also came on Springtime with Neil Watson on a number of occasions.

On one occasion, we found ourselves kedged with no wind and tide against us just off the Castle. We sent a message that we would like a glass of port. The steward Higgins came out in the Squadron Launch with a decanter of port and three glasses on a silver salver. This caused a lot of amusement.

One Cowes week, in the early 70s, I was asked to look after Prince Michael of Kent. We took him to all the parties. John Ingledew, our partner in Dominica was without wife as Caroline had run off. He flew his aeroplane down to Bembridge and brought Lady Christina De La Rue, wife of Sir De La Rue who spent all his time fishing, shooting, and hunting and did not leave the Borders where they lived. She was a well-built, good looking Swedish blonde. She abandoned John and set her cap at Prince Michael who was taken with her.

At the Squadron Dinner on the Friday night, I asked him about Christina. He said he found her very attractive and great fun but not the sort of girl you take home and introduce to Mummy. Princess Marina might have been a bit surprised and so I am sure he was right.

During the same Cowes week, Michael came sailing with us. We were dodging down the shore just west of the Squadron when we went aground. Michael asked, what should we do. Without thinking, I said, 'Push us off.' Michael leapt over the side up to his waist in water and pushed us off before climbing back on board. When I got back to the Castle after sailing, I was taken to task for getting a prince of the royal blood to climb over the side and push me off.

Pops and the children went to Bembridge each year, for about six years. I spent as much time with them as I could but usually, our visits clashed with Cowes week so I'd go to Cowes sailing by day. We started in the Spithead Hotel and then borrowed the Berry family houseboat on the mud. We took our dog, Flynn, with us. One night, he had a very bad tummy and made a terrible mess everywhere. We managed to clear it up but had to replace a lot of mats.

Then, with the Darlings, we rented a very nice house from the Abel Smith family. Finally, we did two years in maisonettes on the road where I recollect the children got chickenpox and Pops had a drama with the nanny who she sacked once she had arranged for Nanny Hetherington to replace her.

One year, I did the Fastnet Race with Mongo Park on his Chance 37. I had done a previous one a few years earlier with Neil Watson on Springtime and, of course, the famous one in 1957.

We were competing in the Admiral's Cup and during the earlier races in Cowes week, we raced around the buoys. I was navigating as I was supposed to know my way around the Solent as a Daring sailor.

We were doing very well in one race and were hard on the wind coming to the finishing line off the Squadron. The Cowes week' Royal Navy ship was a large frigate, Bacchante. It was slack water and she was facing the shore. It was a question as to whether we could get around the bow or would have to bear away and lose a lot of ground by having to go around her stern.

I decided we would have to go around the stern when Mungo, on the helm, shouted I have got a strong blow and can weather or go around the front. He went up into the wind but heeled over a bit more so that the top of the mast hit the jackstaff on the bow of Bacchante flying the Union Flag, which fell to the deck. With that, we crossed the finishing line and got a gun as we were third. Tam O' Shanter was registered in Ireland so we put up the Irish Ensign. This was at the height of troubles with the IRA in Ireland. Of course, both the helmsman and the navigator were members of the RYS.

About two hours later the big launch from Bacchante came and found us on our mooring and presented Mungo with the broken bit of the jackstaff mounted on a plaque with an inscription and intertwined Irish and Union flags. It was Mungo's proudest possession.

The Fastnet Race was very gentle with little wind. We were becalmed off the Bishop Rock and on return in Plymouth Bay. On both occasions, I jumped over the side and had a swim!

CHILDREN AND SCHOOLS AND THE
LAST DAYS AT PEMBROKE ROAD

*F*or much of the time we were at Pembroke Road, I was absent overseas until I had pneumonia and had left Mackenzie Hill. Both Amanda and William went to Lady Eden's school in Kensington. Will was the last boy there until he went to Gibbs, which was run by an old colonel. They were very short of money and the pencils were cut in half.

In 1975, there was high drama as we were informed the Eden family had run out of money. The school would close as the property had to be sold. With a few others, I joined a committee headed by Bluey Mavroleon, rich from a Greek shipping family. We proposed to raise money to buy and save the school. Just when we were about to start putting our hands in our pockets, the stock market had improved dramatically and the Eden family told us the school could continue.

I had joined Lloyd's in 1972, and in 1975 my first cheque arrived, which was going to be a huge help over the next few years. It was treated very favourably for tax as most of it was tax-paid capital gains. Income, by comparison, was taxed at higher rates at nearly 90%.

I failed to find a job that suited me. I had long discussions with the Kuwaiti Investment Office about running their worldwide property investments based in London, which would have suited me very well. They then decided I would have to be based in Kuwait, which ended the discussion.

PART III

NORTH BREACHE MANOR

*E*arly in the new year, 1976, my mother declared that she did not wish to spend another winter in North Breache. My brother had had a business disaster, lost his farm in Somerset, and had parted from his wife and was divorcing. Any decision was, therefore, up to Pops and me. We could either say sell North Breache or as my mother made plain was her preference, we could move the family to North Breache.

I was looking for a new role and had a few job offers but none were what I wanted. I was a director of Oddbins, Welland Textiles, Jove Investment Trust, and Casa Pupo, and Lloyd's underwriting was producing regular profits. I had recently resigned from Great American Industries in the USA.

We put our wonderful house on the market, I bought my brother's half interest in North Breache, we converted the garage/stable block into a house for mother and renovated Yard Farmhouse for my brother who took over the running of the farm. There were over 500 acres but it was all heavy clay; more suitable for making bricks than growing crops.

We had two workers, Terry Mansfield who was the senior – his father before him, having been with the family since before the war –

and John Peters, ex-Navy and had served on the Royal Yacht for a time.

My brother introduced a flock of sheep, which he built up to about 600 ewes. Initially, we had problems with the sheep but we then got things right and it was a successful enterprise, unlike the arable, which was a bit short of a disaster. We started a shoot shared between me and my brother. We hired a very young full-time keeper, Jeremy Hobson who stayed with us for nearly seven years before moving on to a bigger shoot and becoming a successful author. He married our nanny/mother's help, Anne, and they had a little boy.

We sold Pembroke Road in June 1976 to the actress, Diana Rigg, and moved to North Breache. First, we completed my mother's house and moved her in and then we started work on North Breache itself. Meanwhile, we lived in Eastlands Cottage on the drive, which had three very small bedrooms upstairs, a sitting room, and kitchen downstairs and a bathroom off the kitchen. It was, however, the hottest summer for years and we lived outside the front door by day until October.

Amanda was ten and had gone to Lady Tryon's school in Wiltshire as a boarder when we moved from London. Will started at Wellesley House in Kent in September so, until Christmas, only Rupert, aged five was at home. We were able to move into North Breache very early in January 1977.

In February 1976, we took my mother to Dominica to stay with us for 2 weeks. My brother Nick also came. Things were getting a bit difficult there and indeed it was our last visit for a holiday. We had a great time and were well entertained.

I took on the small local firm of builders who had done all the work for our and my mother's house. I bought a plot of land in the village and they built a house there, which I sold quite well.

They also took on other small building jobs for third parties, which I priced and supervised. It was quite fun and I learned a lot about building but it never really made any money and I closed it down some years later.

I helped my brother on the farm, especially with drenching, dipping, and lambing the sheep. I was by no means busy with the businesses I was still involved in. It was a healthy life and I regained my strength after that pneumonia.

We were busy and by 1980 we had given up the Daring with Michael Boyle and Peter Vanneck. We'd had a huge amount of fun with our sailing in Cowes. There had been lots of Saturday night parties in the RYS Castle. One evening, we adjourned to the library upstairs and someone suggested we played strip poker. The wife of a very distinguished military figure got to the stage when she had to remove her bra leaving her in only her knickers when it was decided a halt should be called.

In about 1978, I bought about 100 acres from the estate of a neighbour, Lewis Civval, when he died, and then I bought about 150 acres on the way up to Holmbury St Mary. It included a nice house, which I sold on immediately. We were then farming about 900 acres but not making any money!

About four years later, Anthony Bodie, a well-known London property man bought a nice house from Harry Chapman Pincher, the very well-known journalist, which was in the middle of the land bought from Civval. He wanted the land around his house and offered me a price I could not refuse. The Holmbury land did not produce a return and I was able to sell that for another nice profit.

In 1979, we sold Oddbins to Seagrams for a good profit and as a result of the land sales and Oddbins, I had a large capital-gains tax bill. My accountant, Bob Herdman of Grant Thornton, suggested I rolled the gain over into a garden centre. He introduced me to the Gordons who had run a successful garden centre near Farnham. I, therefore, bought Hollyhock Garden Centre in Cranleigh. I was aware that little of the space being used had planning consent for retail.

The first job was to negotiate with Waverley Council and regularise what we were doing. This, I was able to do. The Gordons lived in a house behind the centre, which was part of the property. They were paid a salary, worked full time, and shared in any profits. There were no profits. It was a dreadful business as a stand-alone garden centre.

The premises were glasshouses and stock faded in sunlight and plants died. Everything we sold was seasonal (stock turn was about three times per annum). We had to spend a lot of money on improvements.

We eventually sold the business in 1987 to Notcutts who could make money out of plant sales as they had a big growing/nursery operation. The Gordons were not easy but the saving grace was we sold the house they lived in separately on the basis that they got part of the sale price. It was a thoroughly difficult business but quite fun at times. Amanda and Will both worked there occasionally. I just about got out with a profit.

One interesting time was when we were prosecuted by Waverley Council in Guildford Magistrates Court for illegal trading on a Sunday. I defended us in person and gave the man from the trading standards office a really torrid time as he had been to the garden centre with his family, including small children when he made the sample illegal purchases. As the law stood then, you could sell food, books, and plants but not a watering can. It was ridiculous. You could sell pornographic magazines under the law but not a screwdriver. Every garden centre ignored the law but some councils were trying to enforce it.

Needless to say, we lost but only after the magistrates deliberated for over an hour. As we left court, the trading standards officer said to me he was not going to be put through that again and he was not taking on any more garden centres. We appealed and had another hearing in front of a judge who found against us but made no order for costs so it must have cost the council a great deal more than the fine we had to pay.

In February 1977, we went to Barbados and stayed in a lovely house on the beach at Sandy Lane. This was with Mark and Karen Armitage, who had a weekend cottage 500 yards from our gate; Andrew and Sarah Wates; and Paul and Annette Wates. It was the beginning of a great friendship although sadly both Mark and Karen succumbed to dementia, Alzheimer's some seven years ago as I write this.

That summer, we rented a boat on the Norfolk Broads with the children, and David and Angela Darling came too and rented another boat. It rained nearly every day and David managed to smash the top of his boat going under Potter Higham Bridge despite a notice beside his wheel reading, 'This boat will not pass under Potter Higham Bridge'. We played a lot of Monopoly.

The following year, we decided on a two-week flotilla boating holiday in Greece. We flew to Salonika and then had five hours in a coach to a little port at Volos adjacent to the Cyclades Islands, including Skiathos. After midnight, we went on board our tiny 27-ft boat with a tiny double cabin aft and three small bunks in the saloon. About twelve similar boats were moored adjacent to each other.

In the morning, we introduced ourselves to the next boat, which had a Belgian couple and three children all slightly older than ours who were eleven, nine, and six. I had met him before in the City. Jacques Delacave ran the London Branch of Banque Brussels Lambert and was destined to become a very good friend and colleague.

The following night, after we had spent the day familiarising ourselves with our yacht, we went to sleep and a few hours later Pops woke me as she could hear noises. I got up and discovered Will, aged nine in the water. I jumped in and got him back on board. He had got up to have a pee and, in a daze, had gone on deck and fallen over the side. Thereafter, I tied a rope around his ankle tied to the mast with enough slack to enable him to get to the loo but not on deck.

The following day, we set sail for Skiathos as a flotilla. We had a picnic lunch. Amanda felt a bit sick but the boys were fine. We then had dinner in a restaurant on the island with about fifty grown-ups and children all at one table. This was the pattern for the next two weeks. However, on the second or third day, we were trying to put a line ashore when it got around the propeller. The engine stopped immediately but the bolts holding the engine down sheared and the engine had come off its mountings. We then had to sail everywhere as we had no engine. Will proved an excellent hand and the Delacaves used to tow us into harbour at night when the wind dropped.

On one island, we visited a lone monk in a monastery on top of a hill. He had no English and my Greek was ancient and forgotten. He poured all of us out a glass of ouzo. When he went to get something to show us, Pops and the children emptied their glasses into mine. On his return, I had to empty my glass. I hate ouzo.

The holiday was voted a huge success and Amanda and Will made a number of new friends. The following year we went back to Corfu for a two-week sailing holiday on a Westerly, which was a lot bigger. We chartered bareboat and were free to go where we wished. We then did similar holidays each year for the next seven or eight years, again in Corfu and south, and then Rhodes and Turkey. One year, we combined the Constantine and Spring-Rice families out of Corfu and each family had their own boat. We also got gradually bigger boats and took friends, the Darlings, and friends of the children.

We had settled down nicely at North Breache. Will was doing well at Wellesley House and Rupert joined him there in 1978. Sadly, he was not that happy but he bravely persevered and we let him do so. Amanda was unhappy at Lady Tryon's and came back to join Rupert at a school in Shamley Green and then Farlington near Horsham. From there, she went to West Heath where she had a great time but was pretty rebellious.

In the meantime, my brother had got remarried to a woman slightly older than him, Frisky Briscoe. She proved a wonderful wife to him. They shared a love of horse racing and she was a good stepmother to his daughters Olivia and Gussie. They lived with them at Yard Farm as their mother was incapable of looking after them.

Frisky was fiercely protective of my brother and we sometimes had disagreements about the farm. Socially, we lived slightly different lives. Nick had become joint master of the Chiddingfold, Leconfield, and Cowdray Hunt.

I was elected a member of the Surrey Club in 1977. It was limited to thirty members and they had to be landowners in Surrey, which condition was interpreted loosely. In the same year, I was informed I had been accepted as a magistrate and would join the West London Bench.

We had bought a small flat in a house just off Kensington High Street when we left Pembroke Road. I had been persuaded to put my name forward by Gordon Pirie when he was Lord Mayor of Westminster. I suffered an intimidating interview and my adventures with Mary June Moore and Jeremy Durham Matthews came back as I had been guilty of assault although I was given an absolute discharge. Fred Lawton who had defended us was now a Lord of Appeal. I rang him and he obviously put in a good word for me. When appointed, I think I must have been a bit unique as Old Etonian, Guards Officers with a conviction for assault were pretty rare in the London Magistracy.

Apart from the farm and my little building business, I then got involved with Jacques Delacave and did some quite well-paid consultancy work for him. In the early 80s, we backed a business in Dundee, which had a system for producing very realistic reproductions of pictures. Andrew Valentine, whose business it was and who had developed the process, had obtained the rights to reproduce pictures from the MCC, Jockey Club, Churchill Archive, and a number of private collections. It was a great product and should have sold to hotels, interior designers and others in large quantities.

Sadly, Valentine was unable to make sales and the business ran out of money and we ran out of patience. Valentine said he would sell the business and had a buyer. He needed to pay the current wages. Jacques and I put up the money and, on the way back from fishing in Scotland, I arranged to collect about fifty or sixty pictures, many of which were nicely framed. They were in stock and we bought them at cost value. These were duly delivered to North Breache. The company sadly went bust but Jacques did not want the pictures so I had a large stock to give to my children and away as wedding presents.

By this time, Jacques had left the bank after it was taken over and had an office next to Westminster Central Hall. I took a room with him and we watched the Queen Elisabeth Conference Centre being built.

BACK TO WORK

In 1981, Will passed into Eton and joined Mr Goodman's house. Amanda was causing mayhem at West Heath and would shortly leave and go to a finishing school south of Paris for a year followed by a secretarial course at Queen's Secretarial College in London and a cooking course.

I started a new venture. An old friend, Michael Haslam, was an insurance broker in Lloyd's who placed reinsurances for some travel agents. His idea was to fund an insurance company underwriting the bonds that all travel companies had to put up. He would place appropriate reinsurance.

I put together an investment memorandum and persuaded the Bank of Scotland to make a substantial investment. They were followed by some other institutions. We duly obtained authorisation as an insurer and recruited John Kaye, who had a small tour-operating business and knew the industry, as MD. He also made an investment alongside myself and Michael Haslam. Thus, was born Travel and General Insurance Company.

From the outset, the company was highly profitable and we built up substantial reserves of cash as well as paying ourselves handsomely.

In the late 1970s, I had sold my interest in Casa Pupo to Chinacraft who had a large number of shops. We also found Welland Textiles facing major competition from the Far East in its circular-knitting business. David Darling had not succeeded in diversifying into anything that worked.

We decide to close the company down. We had taken the cash from the Customagic sale out of the company some years previously. We, therefore, sold the knitting and other machinery, the stock, the fittings, and the properties. We paid off the bank and creditors and employees and distributed a substantial amount of cash to the shareholders. David bought one of the small properties and started a garment business, which did quite well.

In about 1978, I joined the board of Alva Investment Trust, which Jacques Delacave chaired. Its role was to invest in unquoted tech businesses. In this context, we acquired a shareholding in a company in Hastings, Nitech Limited. I became a director. It was run by Peter Barker who had developed ground-breaking rechargeable batteries that were ahead of anything else on the market. These were incorporated in a range of torches and other emergency lighting. The company should have been successful but Peter had a persecution complex in as much as he always thought everybody was cheating him. He was not helped by his partner Lori who shared his concerns. The result was anyone who joined the company failed to stay very long and there were always arguments with customers.

Alva was not a success and a few years later was liquidated. I had grown quite fond of Peter and Lori on a personal basis and so I acquired, for very little money, the shares held by Alva and was the proud owner of 13% of the company. In about 1990, Will left the army and was looking for a job and so Peter Barker took him on as assistant to a new sales director who was a real professional and taught Will a lot. By this time, the company was supplying BT, British Rail, the London Underground and the police with torches and emergency lighting. Everything was looking good but then Peter quarrelled with his new sales director who left and everything went downhill.

Eventually, Peter and Lori bought a small farm in northern France and tried to run the business in Hastings from there with one week in three in Hastings. Will left but kept in touch with Peter and so I gave him the shares. Eventually, the business ceased trading and Peter disappeared despite efforts to contact him. I know Will met him and sold the shares back to him a few years ago.

THE FARM

*I*n 1984, we had a family conference. The farm had cumulatively lost a lot of money partly because we had been running a shoot on it but largely because we had a succession of really bad harvests. Our mother still owned most of the land. It was up to mother and me to pay off the deficit, which we did, and our mother divided up the land and cottages between us.

I got some 300 acres inside North Breache Road, Ockley Road, and Plough Lane together with three cottages and Eastlands Farm. My brother got 350 acres and two cottages at Firethorn with the farm buildings there and at Yard Farm.

I opted out of any involvement in farming activities and took on responsibility for the shoot. My brother carried on farming his and my land and started a large horse livery operation in the big barn at Yard Farm. We did a similar small operation at Eastlands Farm. We had developed a very good shoot doing some eight days with bags of between 120 and 200.

Jeremy Hobson had moved on and Alec Bicknell was the keeper, living in Eastlands Cottage. For some years, we used to keep hens in a pen, collect the eggs and hatch them out and then bring them on to poults until we released them. We would sell up to 2500 poults, which certainly provided some good revenue for the shoot account. Then we had two wet summers and we lost a lot of birds on the rearing field in the mud. It was also hard work for a singlehanded keeper and so we gave up and just bought in poults.

With hindsight our equipment was old and we had suffered quite heavy losses all along the way. I had taken on the shoot and was meeting all the costs. I syndicated four guns to Mark Armitage, Duncan Macgowan, Patrick Hedley Dent and Charlie Petre, all good friends and I used to sell one or two days.

I started first Will and then Rupert shooting when they were eleven. They used a double-barrelled 4.10 with no ejectors. They stood in front of me so they had to shoot early. They both became excellent shots.

ANOTHER BUSINESS

*A*round this time, I was asked to join the board of a quoted publishing company, Musterlin plc. Based in Oxford, they owned the Phaedon Press, which was a renowned publisher of art books; a part-works business, publishing and selling booklets on a monthly basis about big subjects such as architecture or medicine, which the customer collected over time to make a complete work. This was a popular genre at the time of which Musterlin was a market leader. They also owned a book publisher in Scotland and another in London.

They had raised some money through a rights issue with a forecast that they had failed to achieve. I was effectively put there by the merchant bank, Smith Newcourt, who had organised the rights issue.

The chairman was a charming man who I had met with Jacques Delacave. He was highly intelligent and the company was stuffed with very clever people with wonderful degrees from Oxford. However, none of them were business people at heart and they did not appreciate that what they were doing was supposed to make money.

I took one look at the work in progress and saw there was something wrong. The figure was enormous and out of proportion to the sales of the business. I discovered that the part-works business was nearly always the product of the work or ideas of an individual as were the art books. Quite often, said individual would get ill or involved in something else and the project would have to be cancelled or put on hold.

The company capitalised all work in progress but never wrote off any of this expenditure on the ridiculous premise that they might revert to the project at a later date. Writing off much of this sort of work-in-progress asset would produce a huge loss. In any case, the long delay between creating a book and publishing it meant that the company was cash hungry and had very substantial borrowings.

We asked the chairman to resign, which he did reluctantly and the board appointed me executive chairman. We developed cash flows and I determined we needed the bank to write off about £3 million of what they were owed and we would have a viable business after posting a huge loss. Sadly, the bank declined to write anything off.

I sold the two book publishers on a trip to New York for quite good money but the auditors became very agitated as the year-end accounts were being prepared and made it clear that the company was technically insolvent. I had no option but to ask the bank to appoint a receiver, which they did. My understanding was that the bank lost £8 million in the end. The outrageous thing was the auditors had signed off the accounts over many years with the fictitious work-in-progress growing ever larger.

Smith Newcourt also asked me to join the board of a quoted hospital group, HCC, which had about fourteen private hospitals on the campuses of big NHS hospitals. Effectively, they took over the private beds and some facilities in these hospitals as well as operating theatres but had direct access to the NHS facilities on the same site.

Unfortunately, nearly all the deals they had done with the NHS were done at too high a price and it was proving very difficult for the company to make a profit. Mercury Asset management in the person of Nicola Horlick had some 29% of the shares. She was very keen to do a deal with Denis Sokol, a very loud and fat American who had a private hospital business operating in Panama and a number of other hospitals in the course of construction in the Middle East.

My colleagues and I were not very keen on Mr Sokol but just before Christmas, I agreed to go and have a look at the Panama hospital. I spent two days there and was quite impressed. It seemed a profitable operation although it was early days. The objective was for HCC to acquire Mr Sokol's business for shares to give him a quote. He would then become executive chairman and take the business forward.

We were unhappy but Ms Horlick was insistent he was the man to renegotiate with the NHS and so we reluctantly went along and the deal was completed. As I said earlier, Mr Sokol was loud. He also had a gigantic appetite and would order two steaks for lunch off the menu. Two weeks of trying to work with him were enough and I resigned together with a colleague. I understand he completely failed to renegotiate any deals with the NHS and about two years later the company became insolvent and there was a very messy liquidation.

While we were in London, Pops had got involved with the NSPCC. Thus in 1983, when Amanda was seventeen, she was persuaded by Pops to 'do the season'. They went to tea parties, mainly in London and we agreed to have a dance at North Breache in July.

First, however, was something called the Berkeley Dress Show whereby the better-looking girls doing the season, about twenty of them, modelled for a fashion show at the Berkeley Hotel and the other girls sold programmes. It was all in aid of the NSPCC.

Pops announced that she was going to be chairman in 1983 and that she would be moving it to the Savoy Hotel in the evening as opposed to the previous afternoon event. Our favourite gardener, Monty Don, had a jewellery business before he took up gardening and he loaned all the jewellery for the girls modelling. Amanda was a model and Pops' most difficult job was to persuade the mothers of the girls not modelling that selling programmes was much more fun. Nobody could have done this better.

163

✳

Amanda went to many parties while doing a cooking course and we had a wonderful party in July. It was half and half our friends and young. Local people gave dinner parties and we had a live band, Lord Colwyn's Autocrats, and a discotheque. It was one of the finest and warmest evenings and nights I have known. Pops and I were still dancing, together with Mikey and Fiona Spring Rice, at 6 am as the sun was rising and shining into the splendid tent.

IRISH GUARDS

*I*n 1972, I was telephoned by Giles Allan who was commanding the 1st Battalion Irish Guards and asked whether I could come to Regimental HQ, which was in Westminster as Wellington Barracks was being rebuilt.

I met him and Col John Head who was the regimental lieutenant colonel. They asked me whether I would like to become a regimental trustee. Brigadier Denis Fitzgerald was a trustee. He had retired from the army and had joined Panmure Gordon stockbrokers as general and office manager. The other trustee was Desmond Reid who was deputy chairman of the Prudential and chairman of a Lloyd's broker. Retiring as a trustee was another member of the Fitzgerald family.

The job of the trustees was to manage the portfolio of investments held by the regiment. The problem was, John and Giles told me, Denis Fitzgerald spent the meetings pontificating on shares, which he knew nothing about. They wanted a trustee who would stand up to Denis and tell him when he was talking rubbish. They thought I would be ideal to do that and they further told me they were confident I did know what I was talking about. First, John Head and then Giles had been senior subaltern when I joined the battalion as an ensign so I suppose they knew I could be outspoken.

It was a huge compliment and I readily accepted. Remarkably, I had a father, uncle, brother, son and three cousins while Pops had an uncle, brother, and cousin who all served as officers between 1914 and 1990.

About a year later, there was a big Irish Guards party by way of a ball at the Savoy Hotel. People were asked to give dinner parties beforehand and we gave one as we had a large dining room in London. We had about sixteen to dinner, including Mungo Park, Michael Boyle and many other Micks and their wives or girlfriends.

Both Mungo and I were rostered to dance with Elizabeth the Queen Mother, who was very much the guest of honour. Poppity gave us gazpacho as the starter for dinner and so when we arrived at the ball, everyone stood back as the smell of garlic was overpowering. Pops always had a very heavy hand with the garlic.

However, there were no complaints from the Queen Mother when Mungo had his dance with her. A bit later, it was my turn. I had to appear at the top table, wait for a signal, and then ask the Queen Mother whether she would like to dance. Mercifully, she accepted. I remember she chattered away, was very light on her feet, and had rather bad teeth. She thanked me and I escorted her back to her table.

By the middle 1980s, I was the senior trustee, and in that capacity, had the pleasure of explaining all about our investments to the Grand Duke of Luxembourg who, having become colonel of the regiment, wanted to know everything about it.

In 1985, Sir William Mahon became the last serving regimental lieu-tenant colonel as army cuts abolished the role. Henceforth, a senior serving or retired officer would take on the role part-time.

It was decided to form a regimental council that had a much wider remit than the trustees and had a number of senior retired officers on it. I was asked to join as the senior trustee. Initially, it met separately but all three trustees were asked to attend so, after a few years, there were joint meetings. Much later, the use of email and the internet resulted in our reducing council meetings to once a year and trustees meetings to twice.

In 2008 or 2009, Bill Cubitt, a new regimental lt. colonel, decided to change the format of the council and I found out by accident that I had been removed from and had reverted to being just the senior trustee. Bill had failed to inform me of what was happening and I was rather angry. Actually, I was perfectly happy with what he was trying to achieve.

In 2012, the regiment decided we needed more regimental funds to deal with increasing requirements of casualties in Iraq and Afghanistan as well as doing so many things, which used to be done by the army and now had to be done by the regiment. It was decided to start a fundraising campaign with events largely organised by Captain Robbie Wilmont.

We had not done anything pro-active for many years since I'd organised an initiative where we wrote to all retired officers asking them to remember us in their wills or send us a donation. It had secured an immediate inflow of funds and a steady trickle of legacies.

I felt I ought to do something towards the fundraising and so I agreed to walk the North Downs Way from Farnham to Canterbury, a distance of nearly 120 miles. I proposed to do it in five days. I started in Farnham with Amanda and my dog, Otter, for company. We made it to just before Dorking. The following day, Will joined me and we got to Redhill Station, where he got on a train and I went on towards Oxted. There, Pops joined me and we stayed the night with Tim and Sarah Goad, our lord-lieutenant. The third day took me to just beyond Wrotham where Pops and I stayed in a very good Holiday Inn. The fourth day took us up towards Rochester, over the Medway and then to North of Maidstone where Pops picked me up and we went to stay with her sister. The fifth day was a long walk along the downs to Charing at lunchtime. By this time, I had a horrible blister on my left little toe. Also, Pops had been in touch with Robbie Wilmont as they wished to give me a regimental welcome in Canterbury and the following day was the rehearsal of the Birthday Parade on horse guards and so there would be no one to welcome me at Canterbury.

I had lunch and we decided to go home. So, I was only half a day's walk away from Canterbury in four-and-a-half days. We drove back to

Charing the following Tuesday and I had cut the side out of an old pair of tennis shoes so my left toes were showing. Accompanied by Rupert, we did a lovely walk to Canterbury where I was greeted in the early afternoon by the subdean, the Mick Wolfhound and handler, two sergeants in full uniform, and a Mick Piper as well as lots of family.

Otter who had come all the way with me was terrified of the noise of the pipes. The subdean took Pops and I down to the crypt where she conducted a small service of thanks. We then opened some champagne before heading home. I had got myself sponsored and I raised over £35,000 when gift aid was added. I had done my bit.

Anyhow, I soldiered on as a trustee until 2019 when we all agreed it was time I retired at the age of 84. I had done fifty years, three years' service behind the colours and forty-seven years as a regimental trustee. We had a splendid evening at Boodles and I was given a presentation of a desk set suitably inscribed.

LLOYD'S

*L*loyd's, in various ways, has played a significant part in my life from 1971 until the present so, I am covering it all in one chapter. In 1971, Wm Brandts bought a controlling interest in the Sturge Managing Agency at Lloyd's from the Sturge family. I attended the Credit Committee Meeting of National and Grindlays Bank who had to approve the deal as they owned 66% of Brandts.

Lots of senior bankers thought they were buying an insurance company; such was the lack of knowledge of bankers at the time about Lloyd's. Of course, Sturge was not an insurance company as such but rather managed insurance syndicates with others taking all the risk. Reluctantly, they agreed on the deal. Lloyd's is the umbrella over a large number of independent businesses, each of which run syndicates of individual capital providers who enable the managers of the syndicates to write insurance business with the capital providers. These are known as names, and they take the profits and pay any losses once the result of the business written in a calendar year is available after three years.

The directors of Brandts and Grindlays were encouraged to join Lloyd's and underwrite on the Sturge syndicates with at that time unlimited liability. I agreed. It looked an attractive investment and

169

John Hayter who looked after that side of the business at Brandts took me through all the formalities. I duly joined for the 1972 account.

It proved a marvellous investment until 1988. Lloyd's syndicates did not bother too much about making an underwriting profit but rather maximised the inflow of cash by taking on risks, going long into the future for an upfront premium. The resultant cash was invested in government bonds with significant yields, which were bought after half-yearly interest had been paid and sold when pregnant with interest thus creating a capital gain that could be passed on to the names, or investors, as such and either paid no tax or very little tax. In the 1970s, when income was taxed at anything up to 100% this was amazing.

During these years, Lloyd's paid for my children's school fees and holidays. 1986, reporting in 1989, was a particularly good year. In 1988, however, I received a phone call from an old friend, David Lentaigne who had been running Brandts' Insurance, which had become Citibank Insurance. When I left Brandts in 1972, I had been asked to continue as a director of the company for old times' sake!

David asked whether I was a member of Dick Outhwaite's syndicate. I replied it was one of the best I was on.

'Oh no, it is not,' he said. 'Outhwaite has written some appalling risks, which are going to cost the members of his syndicate millions of pounds. This has happened on his 1982 year of account, which he has kept open. I and some broker friends are asking Lloyd's to investigate and we have consulted some lawyers.'

It was early June and David told me they had organised a meeting in the Baltic Exchange in ten days' time and were inviting as many members of the syndicate as possible to see what could be done. He asked whether as a non-working Lloyd's member I would join a committee if it was decided to form one. He assumed I knew more about insurance than I did because he knew I chaired and had started Travel and General Insurance Company in 1980 as well as having been on the Brandts Insurance board and its successors

I could not attend the meeting as Pops, I and others were going to Ascot but, in my absence, I was appointed to a committee. A few days later, we had a committee meeting and I was asked to chair it. The first item on the agenda was finding a chairman. There were lots of people on the syndicate, including Edward Heath, Lord Weidenfeld, Adnan Khassogi, and Robert Maxwell. I carried on as acting chairman and that soon became permanent.

I had sold my interest in James Wilkes and was looking for a new venture. Solicitors Richards Butler, a large City firm, agreed to advise us to see whether we had any remedies.

We needed money and so we thought we would ask all members of the syndicate to send us £100 to join what we called an action group. A list of the names of those on the syndicate and the members' agents' businesses who looked after them was available but not any addresses. Lloyd's refused to give us addresses and were hostile from the beginning. We decided to send a letter to all 1500 members and ask their agents to pass it on.

They initially refused but we pointed out they were bound by the law of agency and they would be in breach of their obligations if they did not pass on our letters. Lloyds agreed and they reluctantly did so and the £100s started to flow in. We paid an out-of-work insurance broker to process the applications in Richards Butler's office. Soon, we had enough money to consult counsel and Stuart Beare, the senior partner of Richards Butler arranged for him, me, and David Lentaigne to meet with Anthony Boswood QC. He had acted against Lloyd's on a number of occasions and felt free to take our case.

At the same time, we went to see Alan Lord the chief executive of Lloyds and told him Outhwaite had written about twenty contracts whereby he acquired the back years of a number of Lloyds syndicates and some insurance companies. This was business often written many years previously and now exposed to asbestos and pollution, which were issues raising their heads in a big way. Outhwaite had taken a premium to effectively reinsure or take on these risks. The fear was that the claims would over time vastly outweigh any premium.

As a result of our pressure, Lloyds asked a QC, Mark Littman, to have a look at the situation. He produced a report, which while being careful not to criticise Outhwaite directly said he had probably been unwise to concentrate so much risk into his syndicate. If it went wrong, the names might have a case for him to answer.

At the same time, Outhwaite reported the open year of 1982 was loss-making and it was not possible to quantify the extent of the losses. He made a call on the relevant names, the members of the syndicate, who had to pay up cash.

This was the trigger we needed to consider legal action. If we were to sue, we had to sue our individual members' agents' companies as through agency agreements they were responsible to us for the actions of Outhwaite. This meant suing all the eighty-four firms of members agents, all of whom had errors and omissions (E&O) insurance so there was a very large pot of money to go against.

Anthony Boswood assembled a team of himself; Michael Crane as junior, later a High Court Judge; and Michael Moriarty as assistant – he was very clever and is now a leading commercial QC. We needed expert witnesses and were fortunate to find Ulrich Van Eichen, a flamboyant German who had run Munich Re's London Office for many years and had a very low opinion of Lloyds' underwriters.

We had to raise money and, by now, nearly 1000 members of the syndicate had joined the action group The 1982 Outhwaite Names Association. I was chairman with David Lentaigne as secretary. We also had a good committee. I had a bit of a coup and Sir John Grenside, a recently retired senior partner of Peat Marwick accountants, agreed to join the committee together with John Tomlinson who was a recently retired senior partner of a leading City law firm.

A maverick member was Christopher Stockwell who later became a total thorn in the side of Lloyds as leader of a totally unreasonable group of names who litigated endlessly against Lloyds. He was a friend and supporter of Dick Outhwaite and told us he was so clever we would never win against him.

I decided to take the whole operation into my home at North Breache Manor with Pat Disley, my part-time secretary becoming full time. We had to get out letters to our membership on a very regular basis as there was no email in 1987 to 1992. I drafted the letters, faxed them to Stuart Beare at Richards Butler who vetted them. Pat Disley then reproduced 1000 copies of the letters and addressed envelopes on an enormous Xerox machine and then it was all hands to the pump, Poppity, our housekeeper and anyone else to stuff and stamp the letters.

My own members agent for my underwriting was Cater Allen. One day, I had a call from them as they wanted to meet with me. I was confronted by a number of directors, including a leading underwriter, Dick Hazell. They told me they would cease to act for me if I continued to sue them. So, I walked out and effectively had no continuing underwriting.

It had been very good for me until Outhwaite and so I was keen to continue to underwrite. Fortunately, I often travelled on the train with Roger Elliot who was chairman of Willis Faber and so I went to see him. He said he would recommend their members agency to act for me. I found James Sinclair who ran it was very sympathetic with what I was trying to do and so I continued underwriting at Lloyds through them.

At the end of 1988, I decided I should try and become an elected member of the Association of Lloyds Members, the ALM, an effective organisation representing underwriting members of Lloyds. I was successful in the ballot as I had started to generate a lot of publicity with my activities on behalf of the Outhwaite Names and there were an increasing number of unhappy names.

I was not exactly welcomed by Anthony Haynes, the Chairman of the ALM who was an ex-chairman of Booker Brothers. He was keen for the ALM to be taken seriously by Lloyds and felt my presence was unhelpful. The ALM had lunches for its members and regional organisers arranged these.

The south of England organiser, John Gooch, invited me to be the guest speaker at an ALM lunch at Goodwood House with about 120 people. I agreed but Anthony Haynes told John to disinvite me as the ALM were trying to get closer to those running Lloyds and I would likely be disruptive. John Gooch was furious. He already had 120 acceptances and their money and so he said it would be his lunch and would I continue to speak. I agreed and I don't think I was particularly controversial.

If we were going to go to court we had to have funding and enough money to pay the costs of the other side if we lost. In the end, we got about £8 million with half consisting of undated cheques from each member.

To set the ball rolling, we convened a meeting in the Methodist Hall just off Parliament Square, which seated well over 1000 people. About 1200 people came who were names on the syndicate, advisers and family members. I stood up and welcomed everyone, telling them what we were going to do. Anthony Boswood spoke and said litigation was always uncertain but we had a case he was prepared to argue. Stuart Beare then explained what was involved. The money started to come in and the show was on the road.

We tried to persuade Lloyds to do something about what looked like being unprecedented losses on the 1982 year. They refused and said we should shut up and pay up. I said we were obliged to pay up but we would not shut up. I and David Lentaigne came under extreme pressure to stop our litigation. At an angry meeting with Murray Lawrence, chairman of Lloyd's at the time, other members of the council, including David Coleridge about to be chairman, and Alan Lord, chief executive, we were told we were a disgrace. Surely, we knew; the risks of underwriting were well-known.

In 1990, I decided to stand for election to the Council of Lloyds. I was successful and with Rona Delves Broughton was elected to serve for four years, starting at the beginning of 1991. We had another meeting in the Methodist Hall with over 1000 people present at which again I spoke together with Stuart Beare and Anthony Boswood who authorised the issue of writs.

Throughout 1990 and 1991, we had all the preliminaries to a trial with writs issued with particulars of the case, which were then refuted by the other side.

Murray Lawrence wrote to all the names on the syndicate urging them to not follow Nutting and be involved in the writ with some veiled threats. This was an anxious time and a small number of working members of Lloyd's and City grandees did withdraw but the majority stayed firm and we proceeded.

I was approached by an assistant to Robin Leigh Pemberton, governor of the Bank of England. He asked me to come and see the governor as he was worried by the publicity the case was attracting and the damage to the City. Having ascertained the purpose of the meeting would be to ask me to stop our litigation, I politely declined to attend.

In June 1990, I had to have my gall bladder removed, which was done in the Lister hospital.

Things were hotting up with the case and a lot of journalists were taking notice. I had hired Simon Morgan, a PR consultant to generate as much publicity as possible. A week after the operation, I was at home when at very short notice, I was asked to come to a BBC studio near Piccadilly where Susanna Symons was interviewing Alan Lord, the chief executive of Lloyds. He would be interviewed about our lawsuit. It was highly desirable I was present to answer him.

Against doctor's orders, I got into my Range Rover and drove to London where I listened to Alan Lord saying how unnecessary and damaging the action we were taking was. I was then put on the spot by Ms Symonds so I had to be pretty aggressive.

During the next few months, I did many further interviews with journalists and more TV.

Our case was going to rest on expert evidence with Ulrich von Eichen our lead expert. He was German and had run the London office of Munich Re. He had a very low opinion of Lloyds underwriters, was very articulate, and opinionated. He was a potential loose cannon and much hinged on him.

Eventually, the day came in September when the case started in the High Court in front of Mr Justice Mark Saville. I spent a day and a half in the witness box being cross-examined by two QCs which went alright. They concentrated on how much money I had made at Lloyds, which was quite considerable and whether I was not aware of the risks which had been explained to me. I thought it went quite well as Boswood told me those cross-examining were two of the nastiest and rudest men he knew. Be aggressive back to them he told me. Our expert witness, Von Eichen was frankly magnificent. He was in the witness box for three weeks.

Then, it was the turn of the defence. Dick Hazell who had sacked me from Cater Allen was their chief expert. He was pompous and self-satisfied, kicked a number of own goals and was clearly not viewed well by the judge. After forty-nine days in court by which time I was an elected member of the Council of Lloyds.

I was asked to go and see Chairman David Coleridge in his office in Lloyds. With him was Stephen Merrett who was representing the defendants, the members agents. They said they wanted to settle the case and would I sit down with Stephen and work out what would settle it, i.e., how much?

The committee of the action group and our team of solicitors and barristers met and considered what we might expect in way of damages. The position was we were likely or certain to win on liability but a separate trial would then have to take place to determine quantum or how much. We did not know what the eventual cost to us all would be as members of the syndicate. They were currently 150% but we were not to know whether they would work out at nearer 1500% by the end or if that had been known whether we would have been awarded all our losses.

I was given a free hand to negotiate with Stephen Merrett. We had a number of meetings and eventually I got an offer of 450% plus our costs to date. It totalled £120million. I had a 30,000 line on the syndicate so I would get £135,000.

Everyone thought we had done exceptionally well and so we settled for that amount.

There was great euphoria in our ranks until the day after we signed. I went into Lloyds and was greeted with the news that Lloyds intended to snaffle our winnings by getting a court order that the money less the expenses had to go into each member's trust fund at Lloyd's. We also had to repay any stop-loss insurance we had before receiving any cash.

The case went back to Justice Saville who heard the arguments, found in our favour, and awarded punitive costs against Lloyd's.

Lloyd's appealed and won in the Court of Appeal so we had to go to the House of Lords in front of the very irascible Lord Sydney Templeman, known as Sid Vicious, and seven Law Lords.

They found in our favour on the main issue; the money did not have to go into our trust funds at Lloyd's and could be paid in cash to us. They did say, however, we had to repay our stop-loss insurers.

This was a triumph and so we had then to get our accountants to work out a programme to divide the monies between each litigant which would be on the basis pro-rata to each litigant's line on the syndicate.

Having agreed to this, I gave a press conference on the steps of Lloyd's and finished by saying I was off to London Airport for a flight to Barbados. Poppity had gone on before me to stay with Andrew and Sarah Wates, Michael and Caroline Wates, and Ian and Emma Balding in a lovely house. There was to be lots of energetic activity; tennis before breakfast, water skiing at 10.30 am, drinks before lunch, a short siesta, golf at 3.15 pm, drinks at 6.30 pm and dinner at 8 pm. This was a slightly exhausting but hugely enjoyable break of two weeks.

I got back to an atmosphere where names and other action groups believed we had opened a door and Lloyd's were in retreat and would have to settle with the names. A new chief executive had replaced Alan Lord in the person of Peter Middleton. He had been a monastic monk for three years after leaving school and had then gone into business. His last job was running Thomas Cook where he had been very successful.

Also, at the end of 1992, Brian Garraway joined to chair a newly established regulatory board. He was a very tough individual who had run Eagle Star as deputy chairman of BAT. He asked me to be the deputy chairman.

Middleton weighed up the situation and became rather unpopular with the hierarchy at Lloyd's when he started saying the names had a case and Lloyd's would probably have to reach some sort of settlement with them. An organisation was set up on an initiative of Tom Benyon, which was called the LNAWP or Lloyd's Names Associations Working Party.

I was chairman and the brief was to negotiate with Lloyd's on a settlement on behalf of all the action groups, the largest and best organised were the Gooda Walker and Feltrim Action Groups. Many syndicates started to report large losses on things like insurance on reinsurance on reinsurance on reinsurance known as the spiral, which saw a huge loss in 1988 when the North Sea oil rig Piper Alpha exploded together with overmuch insurance of asbestosis and pollution and then Hurricane Andrew in 1992. These issues spawned a lot of action groups, about twenty. Some of them had merit but a number did not.

Early meetings were sensible but there was a clear division. There were first, the sensible people who wanted to negotiate and keep Lloyd's afloat because the collapse of Lloyd's would cause us all great harm and financial loss but were looking to a practical solution. Then there were the wreckers who firmly believed everyone was crooked. They had no interest in keeping the place alive and they were broke anyhow.

Early on there was a very angry meeting and as I was a member of the Council of Lloyd's I was accused of being a traitor, stool pigeon, and worse. A vote of confidence was in the offing and so I resigned very publicly and said the lunatic fringe had taken over.

The noisiest individual was Alfred Doll Steinberg who was chairman of the Gooda Walker Action Group. Not long afterwards, he was replaced by Michael Deeney, a music promoter who proved a formidable names' leader. The LNAWP became increasingly fringe and extreme and was eventually chaired by Christopher Stockwell who had been and was a member of our Outhwaite Action Group. They carried on litigating ad infinitum.

In 1991, I had rather surprisingly been appointed chairman of the Solvency and Security Committee, which was tasked with the very limited controls Lloyd's had over underwriters. It was a very big learning curve.

In 1993, Brian Garraway suddenly died and I was asked to be acting chairman of the regulatory board (RB) just at the time when we were introducing corporate or institutional capital into the market. I had to work with Bertie Hiscox who wanted to get rid of all the names and turn each syndicate into an insurance company. He was marketing Lloyd's to institutions while we on the RB had to make up the rules.

I like to think we contrived to constrain the new capital to an extent that third party or names' capital coexists with institutional capital to this day. In the run-up to the settlement of all the litigation within Lloyd's, known as R and R in 1996, I was chairman of the Names' Rights Group. This was an initiative by the members agents, which negotiated with David Rowland to strengthen and entrench a number of guiding principles whereby names were protected more or less in perpetuity.

In 1994, I turned down board membership of Equitas in order to have another three years on the council at a time when so much was going on. I served from 1995 until the end of 1997 and then on the Prudential Reporting Committee, which was the forerunner of the Franchise Board.

While acting chairman of the RB, I started an initiative to align the capital that supported underwriting with the risk of a class of business. At that time, the same capital was required to support ostensibly low-risk business such as motor insurance and catastrophe business such as hurricanes or nuclear power stations.

By 1994, Lloyd's was in a total mess. One group of names after another won actions in the courts and the losses of syndicates were mounting as they struggled to deal with claims arising from pollution and asbestos business written years ago. A plan was hatched by the Council to bring about a settlement of all the problems which involved putting the bad old business into a separate company which came to be called Equitas.

I won't go into the details but as a Council member, I was aware of how close Lloyd's was to collapse.

A plan that involved settling with the names and sorting out the old years was put forward in 1995. I took a lead in supporting it. It was rejected by the names and so in 1996, another more comprehensive plan was eventually accepted, which was known as R and R. We all had to pay up and I suppose over recent years I had seen no profits from underwriting and written cheques for near £1 million. I did not pay any income tax in those years on my reasonably significant earned income.

I had operated and run the Outhwaite 1982 Names Association since 1989 without being paid anything. I also took in another action group, which I ran with Pat Disley for the Gooda Walker Stop-Loss syndicate, which had insured names against losing money. It was very small but the losses were huge and the Gooda Walker Action Group had refused to incorporate it into their action as it was a different business. The action group was chaired by an Australian eye surgeon and the leading light was Marie Louise Burrows, a powerful lady who was on the ALM Committee. I had a small line on the syndicate.

With R and R in 1996, and having distributed most of the £120 million in 1992, it was time to put the action group to bed. However, we discovered that all the action groups were paying their leaders and committee members. We elected to do the same out of money left in the account and I was voted a significant honorarium. I also got a smaller one from the Gooda Walker syndicate.

In 1998, I converted our underwriting into a limited liability company called North Breache Underwriting Ltd. 1997 and 1998 were profitable years but then we had the Twin Towers terrorist attacks in New York so more losses were made in 2000 and 2001. Those who survived those losses – and many did not – then saw some twelve years of uninterrupted profits. By retaining profits, we built up a big investment portfolio that resulted in the investments supporting the underwriting so our only involvement was as shareholders. Tim Oliver, who largely owned and ran a run-off company Hampden took a contrarian view when no one thought members agencies had any future and had bought up one members agency after another, including the agency where Nigel Hanbury and I had been directors. Tim asked me to be chairman with Nigel as MD when I had given up my direct involvements with Lloyd's governance. At one stage we represented nearly 60% of the third-party capital at Lloyd's. I also acquired shares in Hampden Capital, which owned the agency, by providing a bank guarantee at a time when the agency was short of capital. I eventually retired from Hampden in 2011.

My time at Lloyd's led on to a number of other businesses about which more later.

LLOYD'S COUNCIL

nevitably, my involvement with Lloyd's was dominated by the Outhwaite affair.

The Lloyd's Council I joined in January 1991, was very different to today's. Mark Farrer, a senior partner of Farrers – solicitors to the royal family, and a Lloyd's Council member, invited me to lunch before Christmas. He warned me that most members of the council regarded me as having a forked tail and horns.

They did not know me but disliked what I was doing. After all, I was suing nearly all of them in some capacity! He warned me to not be strident and bide my time, which was good advice.

Early in the New Year, there was a huge party on the twelfth floor of the Lloyd's building to welcome and say goodbye to new and departing members of the council. The host was David Coleridge, chairman of Sturge, who presided over a big dinner, masses of flowers, and a string orchestra with the best champagne and wines. Altogether, it was a most extravagant evening. However, I met and found myself after dinner with Stephen Merrett who was a deputy chairman and a very leading underwriter. We got on very well and thereafter, I used to visit him in his office from time to time if I wanted something explained to me as I was flung in at the deep end and appointed chairman of the committee that purported to supervise underwriting in the market. Later, of course, I agreed on the settlement of the Outhwaite case with him representing Lloyd's.

As chairman of Lloyd's, David Coleridge and his predecessors Murray Lawrence and Peter Miller had to visit Lloyd's outposts around the world and, in particular, the USA. These trips were organised as if for royalty. An advanced party preceded his visit to make sure everything would go smoothly. They tested the beds in hotels to be visited to make sure they were not too hard or soft. When the chairman travelled, he took an entourage with him. No expense was spared.

Two years later when Lloyd's was under the cosh of losses, David Coleridge retired and David Rowland replaced him. There was the same party in January to welcome new appointees and say goodbye to those retiring but with many fewer flowers. There was a cabaret after dinner with Kit and the widow. Mary Archer who was a council member and was chairing the Hardship Committee, which dealt with and tried to help those members who were unable to pay their losses, got up in a bright red dress with a plunging neckline and sang a song with the accompanist. It had obviously been prearranged. It was about the problems of Lloyd's and the whingeing names who were causing problems.

It was in the worst possible taste and while a lot of people thought it was funny, David Rowland had a look of thunder on his face and was furious. Mary Archer was a strange character, very cold and measured most of the time. Later that year, I was due to speak at a conference of names in Cambridge. Mary telephoned me and asked whether she could give me a bed for the night as they lived close by.

I said how nice that would be and she said come to supper as Jeffrey would love to meet me. I drove to their house outside Cambridge and banged on the door. Mary answered it and kissed me on both cheeks. She said Jeffrey had sadly been called to London as John Major wanted his advice on something, so it would just be the two of us.

She produced a very good dinner cooked by her and lots to drink and we talked about all sorts of things until after midnight when she showed me to my room and kissed me good night. She was equally friendly in the morning and cooked us breakfast. The day went off well. Two days later I saw her at a meeting in Lloyd's, thanked her for having me to stay, which she ignored and was her usual cold self.

MAGISTRATE

I referred earlier to some problems with my application to become a magistrate.

In 1977, I was appointed to the West London Division of the London Magistracy. There were two courthouses. In Southcombe Street near Olympia sat one of two stipendiary magistrates who sat alone and were lawyers. Cases that involved crime was dealt with here. The other courthouse was in Walton Street near Harrods. Heard here were mainly civil matters such as motoring, TV licences, and family matters but also some crime.

My first day in court was a baptism of fire as I and another newly appointed magistrate, as a result of a muddle, were sent to Hammersmith Town Hall to sit in a court dealing with people who had not paid their rates. My colleague was terrified he might have to say something. He was a very nice man who became a good friend. I took the chair and the clerk told me what to do. It all went well.

We learned on the job. I did about 20 days each year. Early on, I found myself sitting with Dame Shirley Porter, the chairman of Westminster Council, in the chair. I disagreed with her on a case in the retiring room and was promptly told I would see things differently when I had more experience. I very firmly told her my opinion was every bit as good and relevant as hers, which she did not like. She was not an attractive lady and later came unstuck over gerrymandering at Westminster City Council.

On another occasion, we had a burglar who had to be remanded during lunch at Walton Street. He was handcuffed to the radiator. On occasion, I had to excuse myself when young and sometimes old friends appeared in mainly motoring cases. We also dealt with licensing of premises to sell alcohol where I had to excuse myself as I was in the trade as a director of Oddbins.

After some five years, I was eligible to sit in the Crown Court with a judge and another magistrate, hearing appeals from magistrates courts. This happened in Knightsbridge Crown Court where the presiding judge was Judge Friend.

He was known as Judge Fiend as he was a real hanging judge with a terrible temper. One day, I disagreed with his decision, which he was prone to make without consulting the magistrates. He was furious at my temerity to disagree with him, but my colleague rather timorously agreed with me. We overturned the decision of the magistrates and he was purple with fury. Thereafter, I declined to sit in the Crown Court as quite often there was nothing to do when a defendant decided not to proceed with an appeal.

I had some lovely colleagues from all sorts of backgrounds. A lovely West Indian who could see no evil in the most hardened criminal, a union leader involved with the Underground who could see no good in anyone in front of the court, and, in the early days, a number of ladies who had been at it a long time and were absolutely hopeless at chairing the court.

The longest-serving magistrate was chairman of the day. In about 1990, we moved to a new court purposely built in Hammersmith. A regime of training was introduced. There were about eight courtrooms and many more stipendiary magistrates who would later be termed, district judges. It was luxury; a large car park, and a very simple restaurant where we all met up at lunchtime. By now I was regularly sitting as chairman, which made it much more interesting.

One day, I was given a list of cases of motorists who had exceeded 100mph on the bottom stretch of the M1. They had to appear to say why they should not be disqualified. My colleague was a slightly brash very new appointee who said at the outset he had a big BMW and it was only too easy to do 100mph. I told him that was an inappropriate attitude to take into court. The other colleague was a rather mousy lady who did not drive.

The first man in front of us had a very good sob story as to what would happen if he was unable to drive. We accepted his story, did not disqualify him but fined him heavily. The next individual had an equally good story so we let him off. The young clerk started to whisper in an increasingly loud voice that we were not abiding by the appeal court guidelines. I told her we were the decision-makers and we had the necessary discretion. It was all about the definition of hardship or extreme hardship.

I think we disqualified only seven out of a total of about twenty. The clerk took extreme issue with me and reported me to the Lord Chancellor's Office who wrote me a letter admonishing me. ADD

Other colleagues were a very mixed collection, a documentary film-maker who believed the moon landings were a hoax, a successful oil executive, and a very loud lady with a title who discussed the grouse shooting in a loud voice. Time moved on and in 2003, I was asked to chair a specialist pioneer domestic violence court that was being set up and trialled in West London. I had to undergo about three days training and we sat on alternate Thursdays. It was very enlightening and I found it very interesting. Just as I was getting some serious experience under my belt I had to retire in October 2005 after 27 years.

A lot of the work was very tedious but sometimes was very interesting. One such case was a man riding a power-assisted scooter on the road. We had to decide whether it was a car or motor bicycle and so needed to be taxed and insured. We had some three QCs and as many experts on the law but we found it was a motorcycle and so needed to be taxed and insured. The case was appealed but our judgement was upheld and applies to this day.

When asked why I was a magistrate I always said it was so good for me as it provided a window on a world I would not otherwise have seen. It is fair to say that there was a danger you became a bit cynical when you found the same rogues in front of you time and time again.

Also, one had often to hardens one's heart when one dealt with horrendous and sickening matters. Then there were the completely hopeless and disorganised who were always going to be in debt and misery.

My final thought is that the quality of magistrates improved immeasurably over those twenty-seven years. Training and having to be approved before you could take the chair was very desirable.

As a very senior magistrate, I would sit on occasion with a fellow justice who'd aspire to be a chairman. I would let him or her take the chair and judge whether they were up to it or not. If one turned him or her down one had to give reasons, which could be very difficult and greatly upset the individual. Anyhow, retirement brought a glass inscribed paperweight but no letter of thanks.

HIGH SHERIFF

*J*n 1997, I was approached by Corinna Hamilton who was High Sheriff of Surrey and asked whether I would like to be High Sheriff of Surrey. It would be over the Millennium, 1999/2000.

I discussed it with Pops and said yes, although I had not previously been greatly involved in Surrey matters.

Our principle involvement was more Pops than me as she was chairman of Macmillan Nurses in Surrey. She and Anthony and Margery Simonds-Gooding decided to do a Last Night of the Proms in the park at North Breache in September. A large committee was assembled, and we were given a huge stage, which had been used for the Three Tenors in Hyde Park. It was re-erected in the park at North Breache.

The music department from Cranleigh School assembled an orchestra about sixty strong and the Guildford Choral Society of some 150 all fitted on the stage. We got Henry Kelly, a well-known Classic FM announcer, to compère the event with Sue Lawley. I organised the band of the Irish Guards and took charge of the logistics of organising the police and getting the licences.

Pops, Margery and Gill Phillips got together a commercial village of stallholders and bars and food outlets as well as advertising. They also got £60,000 of sponsorship from Cranleigh Freight and the vehicle dealers who supplied their vehicles. We advertised the event widely and invited people to come and bring picnics. Finally, they had to make sandwiches for about 300 people, the orchestra, choir and sound and lighting people as well as St John Ambulance. We included a firework display at the end of the concert and had to warn all those with horses nearby, including Pippa Funnell with her Olympic horses. We had a mass of tents and had to put down some tracking.

It rained in the morning of the day and so I went to Swallow Tiles in Cranleigh who gave me two lorry loads of tile waste, which we put down in various areas in the field which were a bit wet. In the event, we got nearly 9000 people attending, which meant about 3000 cars.

It was a fine evening with a bit of a chill. I went on the stage and welcomed everyone and our triplet grandchildren came on at the end with Pops and Margery and gave flowers to the principal performers.

After the fireworks to Handel's firework music, people started to pack up. The police had organised a one-way traffic scheme and I was told getting out was not too difficult. Afterwards, we went to a tent where we danced to a local band until we dropped.

To the best of our knowledge, this was the first alternate to the Last Night of the Proms on the same night. Thereafter more and more were created. The event made £100,000 for the Macmillan Nurses.

The aftermath was the incredible amount of rubbish left behind. Not only were the designated areas with skips overflowing but there was rubbish everywhere. I had to go to meetings in London the following day but Margery organised about fifteen prisoners from Send Prison who came in a bus, were given bags and lined out, picking the field clean. I had also bought a machine that was towed and had a motor on it, which drove a very powerful sort of Hoover. It was designed for picking up horse poos from smart paddocks but I found it would suck up and pulverise a champagne bottle. This machine worked overtime for days.

My other previous involvement in Surrey affairs was as chairman of the Country Landowners Association in the 1980s. This had been a bit controversial when I was asked to judge the best conversion of farm buildings in the county. I had awarded the prize to a conversion of a chicken farm at the end of the runway at Gatwick Airport, which had been converted into workshop units where about seventy people were employed. Nobody told me that it had been done without planning consent from Mole Valley Council.

There was uproar and, at the AGM, Brendon Sewell, who was on my committee and was chairman of the action committee against the expansion of Gatwick, voted against the adoption of the report and made a speech criticising me. I was asked to go to the Mole Valley and meet the planning committee and then to County Hall in Kingston.

It was around this time I was in trouble with Waverley Council over my efforts to develop in Ewhurst and about using buses at Holly-hock Garden Centre for a restaurant without planning consent. I stuck to my guns and said it was a superb use of redundant buildings and was producing employment.

In a county, the lord-lieutenant is the Queen's representative who is appointed and retires at seventy-five. The High Sheriff is the Queen's representative for law and order and is a one-year appointment. It is today purely ceremonial. In the old days, the judges used to come to the assizes in a county town and the High Sheriff was responsible for their safety and for producing the prisoners to be judged.

So, in 1998, Pops and I went up to London to the High Court where, in a short ceremony, we were nominated as future High Sheriffs. I was going to succeed Richard Stilgoe the entertainer who had among many other things written the book for *Phantom of the Opera*. He was a polished performer and made many of his speeches in rhyming verse. He was going to be a hard act to follow.

Anyhow, April 1999 came to pass and I was inducted as High Sheriff in a ceremony at County Hall in Kingston. I borrowed Patrick Evelyn's outfit of velvet with breeches and sword. I had to buy tights (outsize from M&S), buckle shoes, and ruffs for my neck.

Richard Stilgoe gave a dinner to honour me in County Hall, where he and I made speeches.

I immediately had a very full diary of mayoral receptions, charity events and the *thank you and recognition* business. This meant visiting all sorts of places where amazing people were doing voluntary things.

I think we were perhaps a little more relaxed than my predecessor and we became very friendly with the mayors of Surrey. In particular, the mayor of Spelthorne, which covered the Staines area, became a particular friend and supporter. We did an elaborate ceremony on the River Thames with him and then with the police when the Staines area was transferred from the Metropolitan Police to the Surrey Police.

In July we had a garden party at North Breache. By custom, all the movers and shakers of Surrey were invited. It was a lovely day and we had the band of the Irish Guards playing underneath the big oak tree on the lawn.

The following day we used the tent for a lunch party for about 120 friends. We had considerable involvement with the police. Our chief constable was Ian Blair who was later commissioner of the Met. We got on very well with him and his wife. I liked him as an individual as he was highly intelligent but very ambitious and as a result was politically correct.

His deputy was Peter Fahey who also moved on to greater things in Cheshire and Greater Manchester. A highlight was Ian organising for me to spend a Friday night with the police in Guildford. I was told to wear a white shirt, dark trousers, and a black tie so I looked like a policeman. We had a fascinating evening arresting people passing drugs in the nightclubs and picking inebriated boys and girls off the pavement.

Most of Guildford, which had an enormous nightclub business, was covered by CCTV and this was closely monitored. We arrested one very drunk driver but had to wait some time as there was no breathalyser in the car! It was a fascinating evening.

We made a lot of visits to places where wonderful people were giving up their time to do things that helped their communities. A highlight was the High Sheriff's awards for enterprise held at a big ceremony in Esso's offices outside Leatherhead. Before this, we'd visited a number of projects carried out by young people and had to judge whether they were eligible to be finalists.

The previous year had been a year of literacy with prizes awarded for the schools doing best in that subject. I thought a year of maths would be a suitable successor and so I got some sponsorship and awarded cash prizes to schools that had the most students doing maths for GCE and A levels. In awarding the prizes, I visited some very good state schools in Surrey. School visits were popular and I went in full uniform, showed my sword, and told them what High Sheriffs did.

I worked out that I wore the full uniform on thirty-five occasions during the year.

The summer was quiet but things hotted up near Christmas and the Millennium. We spent a lot of time in Guildford Cathedral where I read a lesson and had become good friends with the bishop, John Gladwyn. The New Year was busy as it was the period up to leaving office in March. We had got on very well with the mayors and had entertained them all with their wives either to dinner or lunch when we gave parties for local people mixed with our friends.

Near the end of our year, we were told the mayors wished to give a dinner for us. We understood this had not been done before and so we attended a party in our honour at a hotel near Woking. It was a very enjoyable evening and subsequently, for about six years the Millennium mayors of Surrey met for dinner or lunch and invited us every time. One Sunday they came to us.

At the beginning of April, my year was over and so I gave a dinner at County Hall to welcome my successor Michael More Molyneux and his wife. Fifteen years later, he became lord-lieutenant of Surrey and is still doing a great job. One individual pricked, for that is what the Queen does to a list given to her with names of potential High Sheriffs, using a bodkin, withdrew as he decided it would be too expensive, and so I had to nominate someone to replace him.

Sarah Goad, our lord-lieutenant, who with husband Tim became very good friends, asked me to nominate Penelope Keith, the very well-known actress who was a great doer of things for Surrey. At that dinner, I gave a resume of the eventful year in mine and Pop's life. It was my job to nominate someone to be High Sheriff in three years' time. I approached Andrew Wates who was very involved in the family business. He was initially a bit reluctant. However, he came round to the idea and when his turn came, he was not only a very good High Sheriff but it launched him into many aspects of Surrey life where he got very involved. Our year was over and so we went off to St Lucia for a well-earned holiday.

HOLIDAYS AND CHILDREN

I now go back in time. Up until 1976, when we moved to North Breache and Dominica was happy, we rarely went anywhere else. In 1978, we went to Barbados with two Wates and Armitages. The next year, we went to the Maldives for two weeks via Sri Lanka with Charlie and Mel Petre. The two of them and I learned to scuba dive.

It was not for Charlie although he persevered. He went down and then came up again saying, 'I was not born a fish.'

My buddy was Susan, a rich, plump girl married to the local golf professional. He and Pops stayed onshore. We then found Montserrat in the Caribbean, a beautiful island that was still a Crown colony.

We stayed in a small hotel and then the following two years we rented a lovely house from a local. There was a lovely golf course, about twelve holes, and then you did a few more from different tees to make eighteen. Our house was built into a hillside and overlooked the twelve and eighteen green. We had Amanda's husband, James, with us and other friends.

We came back the following year and in one of the years, they had an open golf tournament. I won the seniors, which was for over fifties and James was the runner up in the main event.

We made good friends with the governor who we called Sid from Sidcup.

The chief of police was a former superintendent with the Sussex police who said there was no crime on the island. It was a population of 12,000 and he knew all the rogues. Perhaps that was the case as one of our party left his wallet with money in it on the counter in a shop in town. An hour later it was delivered to our house by taxi!

Montserrat had a defence force and due to some of the early settlers being Irish, they had a relationship with the Irish Guards. Indeed, a number of Montserratians had joined the Micks as recruits. When they discovered I was a trustee of the regiment and as we were there in March over St Patrick's Day, they asked me whether I would take the salute at the parade they were having. I gladly accepted and did so wearing a rather scruffy Panama hat and my boating jacket. Those on parade were from both sexes and varied from a smart 6 ft 3 in man to a vastly fat seventeen-year-old. We then had a drink afterwards in their mess.

Sadly, there was some concern about the volcano being a bit active. We drove up as far as we could and there were lots of sulphur springs. We could have taken a helicopter to have a look in the crater and we were told it all looked a bit active. Of course, some months later there was a huge eruption and the town, our house and the golf course were covered in 20 ft of lava. One side of the volcano collapsed and permanently put the small airport out of action. It was a major disaster, many of the population left, and much of the island is uninhabitable to this day.

In 1986 and 1987, Amanda had been working for Drexel Burnham, a leading investment bank, on the dealing desk with some pretty hard cases. She had done so well as aged nineteen she was being paid £1000 for each year of her age. It was a hard life for a girl, and so she decided to have a gap year and flew to Thailand with a girlfriend.

We went out there to meet her in Bangkok, staying in the Mandarin Oriental. Amanda and friend were in a backpackers hostel not far away. We had booked rooms in a lovely hotel in Koh Samui. We set out to the airport to catch our booked flight only to be told at the airport that our plane had been commandeered by a government minister. There were no further flights that day and the following day's only flight was already overbooked. It was also Easter. What to do?

We found a taxi and the driver agreed to take us by road to the little port where we could get the ferry to our hotel. It was about 250 miles and expensive. We set off at about 10 am and got to the ferry at about 6 o'clock just in time to catch the last one. Our travel agent reimbursed the cost.

Sadly, the swimming was disappointing as the water was very cloudy from the river nearby. But we had a lovely week.

We came home and Amanda got a job on a yacht. She would ring in every week to let us know she was safe. Then we heard nothing for about a month and started to get worried. We contacted the consulates in Bangkok and Phuket and then the Foreign Office. We were about to go out to Thailand when Amanda called. They had sailed down to Singapore and could not go ashore in Malaysia, so she could not call us. These were the days before mobiles!

She continued on her travels and spent quite a lot of time in Tokyo. When she returned, she got a job with Mark Cannon Brookes and Christopher Lyttleton at NCL stockbrokers.

She stayed there until after she got married to James Thornton in 1990 at North Breache. We had a large wedding in Cranleigh Church with an Irish Guards band, followed by a reception at North Breache and a party afterwards.

She never really fancied James when she first knew him but he spoilt her rotten. He earned a lot of money and was pretty flash. He was the head of foreign exchange at Shearson Lehman. Then suddenly she went to the south of France with him. We got a call from Amanda that James had proposed and she had accepted. She implored us to come out to the Hotel du Cap in Cap Ferrat where they were staying. It was a ridiculous hotel for the very rich. We were a bit dubious but went and I remember paying for a preposterously expensive dinner in a nearby restaurant.

In 1986, Will left Eton. He had done very well. He was also a very good head of house, and for this, I had given him a little Toyota when he passed his test which he did fairly quickly. He kept the car in a car park off Eton High Street and I later discovered used it to get to London for parties.

Prior to his final year, he had had an unsatisfactory career and some very unsuitable friends. He sat his A levels and the results were just short of disastrous. He would not have got into any sort of decent university. We had been looking at the USA and he had done some SATs where he got quite good marks.

We decided the army was the answer and he was accepted by the Irish Guards. They did not want him for nine months and so he went off to Kenya. About five months later, they did want him and so he came back. He had put on a lot of weight though and, of course, he was asthmatic. The latter was a no-no for the army and so he had to hide that. He failed his medical for being overweight. He was given another chance in three weeks' time but had to lose nearly 20 pounds. He succeeded by not eating, masses of exercise, and dehydrating. Thus, it was off to the Brigade Squad at Pirbright.

Rupert went to Milton Abbey in 1983 where he initially hated it as he was small and overweight and got a bit bullied. Before that, we went for an interview at Harrow, which was not a success as Rupert was asked what was the most recent book he had enjoyed reading. He stumbled and, on an inspiration, said *The Day of the Jackal*. He had seen the film. On being asked what it was about he was speechless.

I then blundered by referring to the housemaster who interviewed us as Mr Outram when he was a baronet! After his GCSEs, which were not great, we decided to remove him in 1987. By that time, we had a flat in More Close near Olympia. Amanda and Rupert had over a year there together. She was studying for her stock exchange exams and Rupert was at MPW, a crammers, doing his A levels.

At this time, our great friend Rudolph Agnew was chairman of Consolidated Goldfields who had a conference centre in Somerset at Mells Park. He used to ask me and the boys every Christmas to stay and shoot after Christmas as he and Whitney his wife used it as a second home. Great quantities of pheasants were shot by me and the boys with the Scholeys, Petres, Wiggins and Cairns boys.

FAMILY AFFAIRS

$\mathcal{B}$y 2002, I was working a bit less. I still chaired Telecom Plus which was doing well and Hampden Agencies, which was also doing well. Lloyd's was starting to make money again. I was on the board of Jove Investment Trust. Poppity was doing her Macmillan Nurses in Surrey and London and had joined the committee of the Cranleigh Village Hospital Trust. The Trust had been gifted about three acres of land in Cranleigh by Nick Vrijland and proposed to build a nursing home/hospital with some twenty free beds for local needs.

Around this time, I was also asked to join the board or committee and become chairman. I got very involved and we had a deal ready to go with a property company who financed and built hospitals, which were then run by the NHS and the local doctors. I spent many hours on the transaction when suddenly the local doctors pulled out, which derailed the whole project.

As far as family was concerned. Amanda had married James Thornton in 1991 with a big wedding at North Breache. In 1995, she gave birth to triplets, a boy and two girls. They were small but very healthy. James and she were not particularly happy. He always spent more than he earned and I had to bail them out. As a result, they sold their Fulham House and moved to Plough Farmhouse where I did him a very favourable deal. James was never interested in his children and the marriage went from bad to worse when on a whim he bought a necklace from Garrard's. This had been lent to and worn by Princess Diana on what turned out to be her last public engagement before her death. He paid £250,000 for it, which he did not have. £50,000 was payable to the Prince's Trust and so the necklace itself, which as a necklace was worth less than £100,000, was quite expensive.

I declined to finance him but one of the people who had worked with him in the City put up the money for a half share. They kept it for over a year and then organised a special sale in New York to which very few people turned up. It was sold for a sum that just about covered what they had outlaid. Prior to the sale, James and Amanda were invited to a dinner at Highgrove in thanks for the generous gift to the Prince's Trust. James got very drunk and was boasting how he had so much money he did not know what to do with it.

After that and the failure of the sale, James lost his job and they parted with Amanda suing for divorce. James said he would not be seen for dust after he was divorced and put up a considerable fight, which just cost a lot of money.

True to his word, he went off to Switzerland, abandoned his children, and never paid the child maintenance that the court had ordered.

Will left Eton and spent his four years in the Irish Guards in mainly Berlin when the Wall came down. He did a variety of jobs after the army, selling torches for Nitech, glasses from Czechoslovakia for a friend, jodhpurs for David Darling, and finally Simon Horn beds.

He then decided to go into the City, firstly with Flemings and then two small firms before joining Bank of America.

In 2000, he married Lisa Wilmot, a very pretty and sugary girl from a well-known commercial family in Canada. The wedding took place on the Lakes at Muskoka where the Wilmots had a large house called a cottage and a boathouse with a collection of motorboats. We and a number of our friends were royally entertained over a whole week. There was lots of golf and speeches. Michael Wilmot could never resist making a speech and nor could his daughter. After a service conducted by the Bishop of Toronto, there was a big reception and dinner/dance with Galen Weston making the speech.

Afterwards, we, the Darlings, and Armitages flew to Alberta where we hired a car. We drove to Banff, then up the Ice Highway to Jasper where we played golf and I went white water rafting. It was grade six and we went over considerable rapids. I was thirty years older than anyone else on the raft. We then went to Whistler where we went riding in the Rockies, which was very special, and played more golf. We finished in Vancouver and then flew home.

On our return, we gave a large dinner-and-dance party at North Breache and entertained many of the Canadians. By 2002–2003, they were living in a lovely house on Wandsworth Common and Will was doing very well working very hard at Lehmann Brothers. They soon had a daughter, Emily, and two years later, Sophie. They lived in considerable style with a nanny and a daily lady so they could go away on holiday as often as Will's job made possible. We were very friendly with the Wilmots who spent a lot of time in London, staying with Will and Lisa.

They spent two Christmases with us at North Breache and came as our guests to Achentoul for a week. They then asked us and Michael and Fiona Spring Rice to come and stay with them in their house at Windsor in Florida. On arrival, they suggested we would be more comfortable in the resort guest house. We had a very jolly and enjoyable week with lots of golf and parties. A highlight was Michael Spring Rice and I being flown down to the Tournament Players Course (the TPC) where we played that very difficult course with Michael Wilmot and a friend of his. Sadly, we left with a slightly nasty taste as we were presented with a large bill on our departure!

In 2003, Rupert married Kerry from Northern Ireland and we had the wedding at North Breache. They lived in the lodge at North Breache. Rupert was working as a diesel mechanic and Kerry, as a qualified barrister, was working for the Crown Prosecution Service. Two years later they had Charlie. I had by now given the lodge to Rupert as I relied on him to do a lot with the estate.

TELECOM PLUS

$\mathcal{A}$fter I had sold out of Travel and General, I was introduced to a small insurance company, IGI Insurance Company which had all the licences. I expressed a strong interest and then discovered they were also talking to some South Africans. To cut a long story short I joined forces with Clive Saron, John Levin and Ari Kremeris. I became chairman and Clive was MD. He had a lot of insurance broking experience in South Africa but had got caught up with a scam involving ABSA Bank and fallen foul of Lloyd's. IGI had a Lloyd's facility and so it was agreed I would buy this from the company which worked well as an arrangement. I had an office at IGI next to Lloyd's and with my partners, we developed the business successfully, with a few bumps in the road from time to time.

One day in 1997, I was sitting in my office on Lime Street when one of our people asked me whether we would pay £10,000 to sponsor a polo match at Tidworth. My fellow shareholder/directors were away and I said No. Twenty-four hours later, I was asked whether we would do it for £7500. They were very keen to do this and I agreed.

Pops and I drove down to Tidworth and met Richard Elliot Square, an ex-army officer who was organising the polo. My colleague John

Levin was also there. It was a match of the army v the navy with Prince Charles playing for the navy.

They won and Pops presented the Cup to him. While watching the match, Dale Tryon, a former girlfriend of Prince Charles, who we knew and who was getting rather eccentric tried to talk to him. He said to me, 'For goodness sake, please, keep that crazy woman away from me.' We succeeded in doing so.

We got quite a bit of publicity out of the event, which was worthwhile.

However, John Levin and Richard Elliot Square got involved in Richard's idea of an alternative supplier of telephone services as a result of the opening of competition to BT. His idea was to use a commission-only sales force on the pattern of Avon Cosmetics and some very successful at that time, jewellery businesses.

They had got a long way down the road of raising £1million with a quotation on the OFEX exchange with a prospectus in draft form when they approached me as to whether I would be chairman. The idea seemed a good one but I had doubts about some of the people. I agreed after I was told the brokers they were using had said it would be a doddle raising the money.

The prospectus was finalised and marketing began with institutions. This was done by Richard and was a pretty good disaster. They had about £400,000 and then got stuck. I persuaded Mark Cannon Brookes at NCL to put up £350,000 from private clients and an investment trust I was a director of put up £75,000.

To get over the line, I put up some £50,000 and we just scraped to £1million.

To make the system work, we sold a customer a box that was attached to the telephone and was diverted to us. A deal was done with a supplier of those boxes. Offices were taken near Henley and within six months, we had proved the concept worked.

We had a significant number of customers but we had run out of money. I had a very anxious Christmas 1997 and decided Richard had to go and two other directors who were not delivering. They all had substantial carried interests, which I persuaded them to reduce.

We then started to talk to potential partners some of whom, like

Ericsson, showed interest. Then, I was introduced to Charles Wigoder by Richard Michell, our finance director. Charles had started Peoples Phone, a mobile supplier and a forerunner of Carphone Warehouse and Phones 4 U. He was backed by venture capitalists and the business was very successful. However, he fell out with his backers and resigned. They had great difficulty running the business without him so it was sold to Vodafone. Charles still had his shares and so got about £10millon from the sale. He had been looking for a new venture in telecoms.

He drove a very hard bargain but had to give a large shareholding to the crucial supplier of the boxes who had never been paid. He put in £1million of his own money by way of a deeply discounted rights issue and became chief executive. He asked me to stay as chairman and John Levin as a non-executive together with Richard Michell, the finance director.

We subscribed in the rights issue but the founders were more or less wiped out as they were not invited to subscribe to the rights issue. New premises were taken off the Edgeware Road and Charles started to recruit his old team from Peoples Phone. We had further rights issues, to all of which I subscribed as I found I had increasing confidence in Charles and his team. He did not suffer fools gladly and was arrogant but he was always focussed.

I enjoyed working with him. He was totally different. He owned a bridge club near Marble Arch and his ambition was to play bridge for England. He was also a poker player and would go off to Las Vegas and play poker for a week. We added mobile phones to the fixed-line service for our customers and then broadband. This was followed by getting licences to sell electricity and gas. Everything went onto the same bill. We then made an investment in Oxford Power, which was a management buy-out of Enron Direct when Enron collapsed in the USA,

The business prospered but we felt we needed a higher profile for it. We decided to get a quote on the London Stock Exchange and did so in 2002. Our method of marketing precluded advertising so our customer acquisition costs were very low. It was word of mouth by our commission-only sales force. In 2005, we suddenly found ourselves selling gas at 40p a therm, which as a result of a sudden spike in whole-sale costs was costing over 100p a therm. This was a sure road to bankruptcy.

We called in Rothschilds and finished up transferring all our energy customers to nPower, one of the Big six suppliers with a contract that insulated us from price movements in wholesale markets. In return, nPower acquired a very large customer base without any debt risk or billing costs. We entered into a long-term contract that provided us with a satisfactory margin. This then allowed the business to start growing again.

As each year went by, we reported increasing profits and a growing share price. In 2011, I had to get heavily involved with our shareholders and issues surrounding corporate governance. Having sorted any prob-lems out with our largest institutional shareholder, Standard Life, I decided I ought to retire. Charles was keen to take over as chairman and so I squared this with the major shareholders. Charles then asked me to organise a number of changes in the board with two directors also retiring with me. So, I duly retired from the company at the AGM in 2012.

Thereafter, the company's growth faltered as a mass of new compa-nies entered the energy market, offering very low prices but very bad service. After I had gone, they also paid nearly £200 million to buy back the customer base from nPower after selling the stake in Oxford Power for some £65 million. This improved margins but gave rise to a lot of goodwill on the balance sheet, which has to be written off.

I am sure it was the right thing to do but competition slowed the company's growth and the shares stagnated moving between £9 and £15, having reached £19.50 at one stage. The shares are in the FTSE 250 and the market capitalisation is well in excess of £1 billion which is pretty good for a business started from scratch in 1997.

Both Pops and I put shares into trusts for our grandchildren when the shares were around £3 and I also put shares into my charitable trust, which I had originally set up many years ago. As I write, the govern-ment capped the tariffs of all companies and many of the new entrants to the energy market went bust when there were big moves in whole-sale prices. The regulator has also, far too late in the day, tightened the criteria required to get a licence to sell energy.

They have nearly 700,000 customers, a majority of whom take three or more services and own their own houses so both the bad debt levels and the churn of customers is very low for the industry.

PART IV

LAST YEARS AT NORTH BREACHE

*I*n 1999, my brother decided to give up farming, retire, sell up and move away to somewhere near Lambourne where he and his wife, Frisky, had so many friends. He had given up hunting after a dreadful accident when he landed on his head and was lucky not to break his neck. He was in a brace and could not ride for 18 months. When he did, he found he had lost his nerve. He had been master of the Chiddingfold, Leconfield and Cowdray Hunt for twenty years.

He also had prostate cancer, which was successfully dealt with and he is very fit today in his eighties. He had a very large livery yard at Yard Farm, which made a bit of money but farming sheep and anything else on the Wealden clay of North Breache was very difficult.

They bought a very nice house in Shalbourne near Marlborough in a village with an unusual number of nice people.

My brother sold his 150 acres and the farm buildings very well to John Mitton, who was Frisky's stockbroker and a keen hunting man. He had a very frightened mini wife to whom he was clearly not very kind.

I was left with some 400 acres, which had always been mine, but no urge to farm it. Fortunately, Rupert was living in the lodge that we gave him. He took an interest in the farm. We increased the number of stables to over twenty, built a sand school and a girl called Nicky Lithaby ran a livery stable there with Rupert and Poppity overseeing what went on.

Meanwhile, my mother in her mid-nineties was still fit and living in Stable Cottage behind The Manor with her nice garden and Labrador, which came out shooting with her. She had, however, completely run out of money. She cashed in her last investments as she had never expected to live as long and had given everything away to my brother and me. I owned her house.

I gave her money each month. She was very careful of the allowance I made her, and I organised quite a lot of financial help from the council, particularly to pay for carers as Mother needed an increased amount of help. She could still cook very well and entertained Pops and me to dinner at least once a week and sometimes more. We included her in everything. My brother contributed his fair share as best he could. This situation only occurred because of her extreme generosity earlier. She never thought she would live to be 100. She got her card from the Queen.

Our finances became very difficult around 1987 when Lloyd's started to make heavy losses and we had to write large cheques each year. Pops decided to go into the corporate entertaining business. We had corporate days when companies came and carried out activities in the park. This often included lunch in the dining room.

We had weddings in marquees on the lawn. Later on, Rupert and I constructed a 4x4 cross-country course in the woods. At one stage, we had Americans to dine and stay. I vetoed this after a few times as the last thing I wanted was to get back from London after a difficult day and find I had to make conversation to a whole lot of strangers.

We even had a murder evening with actors, which was quite entertaining. All this made a bit of money and was hard work for Pops on top of her charity work, mainly for Macmillan Nurses where she was chairman for Surrey, and actively involved in London creating and organising events.

In Surrey, she led a fundraising to successfully build a daycare centre for Macmillan in Guildford. It was, however, a lovely surprise when she was awarded an MBE in 2002 for her charitable work. Three of us, me, Rupert, and Amanda accompanied her to Buckingham Palace where she was given her medal by the Queen.

In the mid-eighties, I had the idea of getting planning consent to build some houses on about three acres of land that I owned jointly with my brother. It was adjacent to the main road in the village of Ewhurst.

At that time, the village was keen to rebuild the village hall. I needed support for a scheme so I offered to build a new village hall with car parking on part of the land if I took the old village hall and I was allowed to build twenty-two houses on the rest of the land. I was shouted down and accused of trying to bribe the village. I then decided to just go for planning consent and I got plans prepared for a development of some fifty houses. We were turned down flat by Waverley Council and so we decided to appeal.

In the meantime, my good friend Sir Michael Creswell who was our local district councillor died. He had been a huge help in getting the uses of the garden centre regularised. For years, he had been returned unopposed as an independent. I decided to stand in the ensuing by-election for the Conservatives. That was not difficult as I was chairman of the Ewhurst Conservative Association.

Party HQ in Guildford only very reluctantly agreed to me being the official Conservative candidate especially when I said one of the planks of my appeal to voters was the need for more and cheaper housing for local young people. I was opposed by a perfectly nice man who was severely crippled as a Liberal Democrat. He made much of my plans to develop houses in Ewhurst and all my mother's friends were very opposed to the development.

Poppity and I campaigned hard and called on nearly all the houses in the village. I was confident I would win but I was ignominiously beaten by the Liberal Democrat. I was not that sad as I had made my point about housing and would have only served for about six months as there was an election for the whole council coming up. I was certainly not that keen on being a local councillor. Also, this was just before the Falklands War and the Conservatives under Mrs Thatcher were very unpopular in the country.

Anyhow, we went to our planning appeal after we had an open meeting in the village hall and got a lot of support from many of the older families in the village whose children had no chance of ever owning a house locally where they had been brought up.

The inspector sat for four days and we made a good case but were not that confident. His deliberations were inconclusive but Nicholas Ridley, the responsible minister, gave consent and to the fury of Waverley Council we had outline planning consent.

Then, serious discussions had to take place for the next year. Surrey County Council claimed to own a ransom strip that could deny us access as they argued we only had agricultural access through our gate on to the road.

We were advised to settle and paid them £250,000. At the same time, Waverley remained astonishingly obstructive and held us up from getting details approved by imposing all sorts of conditions on us. By this time in the late 80s, there was a recession and the market was not good. I needed the money as Lloyd's was costing me very dearly and Brother Nick was also keen for some cash.

In the event, we sold for about £1 million for forty-four houses of which eight were low cost. We also kept one house. The time between me proposing the village hall idea and getting money into our pockets was 10 years.

In 2001, my friendship with the Bishop of Guildford resulted in him asking me to accompany him and a small party to Nigeria. The Guildford Diocese has a formal link with Nigeria and I had played a part on getting Ewhurst to retain its own vicar by agreeing that 20% of a new vicar's time should be spent on the Nigeria link.

It was a fascinating trip, which I wrote up at some length. I was asked primarily because John Gladwin was the C of E Bishop in the House of Lords who spoke on sovereign debt and he wanted someone with him who understood more about the subject than he did.

I think I finished up as the cheerleader for the party. The Primate of Nigeria, Archbishop Peter Akinola became my best friend for the duration of the trip. He was incredibly dynamic and nothing was off-limits for discussion even including gay sex, which is, of course, totally unacceptable, and very illegal in most of Africa.

On one occasion, we were waiting for a bishop to arrive in a half-built so-called Bishop's Palace when I got locked in the lavatory. Having shut the door, all the lock fell off outside the door. The door was very strong and I failed to push or kick it down. I shouted but no one heard me. There was a window and after a half-hour, I managed to attract the attention of a local who alerted my colleagues. They had been pretty dozy but thought I had gone for a walk.

We attended church in Ibadan for installing three new bishops. The service lasted four hours but the music was wonderful and a bit like being at the opera.

It was a fascinating country, one of the most corrupt in the world, and very religious. 17 Million C of E attend church regularly and about 20 million Catholics, but they would all steal anything from anybody. There was obviously a very grim situation of Christian v Muslim. There were masses of Saudi money funding the building of mosques and encouraging violence to Christians.

We were entertained by the King of the Yorubas who are about 40% of the huge population of Nigeria. There was a fascinating cere-mony, which was very Nigerian, followed by a lunch of Mulligatawny soup, roast chicken, and lemon pancakes. It was all very English. The king had a big house in St John's Wood. On departure, two live turkeys were presented to us. We finished with a service in the cathedral in Abuja, the capital, where John Gladwyn preached and his wife Lydia and I led a conga round the cathedral. There were 2000 people in the cathedral and another 2000 outside. It was a fascinating trip over two-and-a-half weeks. Fortunately, I had acquired some gin and so we, John, Lydia, and I, mixed it with whatever we could find, often fizzy orange.

SURREY TO HAMPSHIRE

*J*n 2004, my mother was getting very old and was ninety-
nine. One morning, she had my brother and Frisky to lunch
and realised she had no cream. She jumped into her car and went to go
to the village shop. On the way, she crashed at relatively low speed into
the local window cleaner's car. He was up a ladder cleaning windows.
She was a bit shocked but unharmed and little damage was done to
either car but the police and an ambulance were called. Sadly, the
police agreed to take no action if Mother surrendered her licence. She
was very reluctant but accepted the inevitable.

Early in 2005, she was going to be 100. We planned a lunch party
for about 100 and a drinks party for rather more but mainly locals for
the following day. The invitations were printed and we were addressing
envelopes when mother fell in the night and broke her hip. She had a
new hip in Mt Alvernia but we needed care for her when she returned
home. She was certainly able to walk again but it knocked the stuffing
out of her and she started to gradually go downhill over the next 18
months. Instead of the big parties, we had a lunch party for about
twenty with Mungo Park who came over from Ireland and the
Chesterton family. She was Mother's sister.

By 2006 and now 101, Mother was going downhill. Caring for her

214

was becoming increasingly difficult and Pops and I hatched a plan to move her to the care home in the village. That was done in conjunction with a family conference where it was clear none of our children wanted to take on North Breache and the estate. Rupert was working as a mechanic but owned the lodge; Amanda and her three children were living in Eastlands Cottage, which I had improved and extended. Will was married and living in London, earning lots of money

In June, we instructed Lane Fox to sell North Breache, including the lodge, Eastlands Farm and all the land except about 14 acres adjacent to the village in Ewhurst. We were then persuaded to make Knight Frank joint agents. There was considerable interest as the market was very good but people were surprised by the asking price. In the event, we agreed on a sale in early September to a hedge-fund man, Ivor Farman. He proved a very difficult buyer to deal with, was very pernickety but we dealt at near the asking price. We agreed we would not give possession until 17 March 2007, after exchanging contracts late October.

We then had to find a house for ourselves. We hired a 'finder' lady who took us to see Field House, Bentworth in Hampshire. We knew the vendors, Peter and Toni Isdell Carpenter and had been to a bridge evening with them some time previously but had little memory of the house.

The price was sensible whereas other properties we looked at were either totally unsuitable or ridiculously overpriced. When looking at two houses in Sussex, we had an urgent call from the carer to say that my mother was failing. We rushed back and about one-and-a-half hours later, my mother died very peacefully in her bed with me holding her hand. We went back to Field House where two other parties were interested.

I paid a bit over the asking price but my offer was unconditional, not subject to a survey as I had a very good look round the house, which was actually only just over twenty years old. We got possession in mid-January and were able to put builders and decorators in who stayed in the house. Just before Christmas, the Isdells gave a leaving drinks party to which they invited half of Hampshire. They had included on the invitations 'To meet Peter and Poppity Nutting'. Actually, we knew at least half the people there.

We had Mother's funeral in Ewhurst Church with about 200 people present. I wrote a script that Will delivered extremely well. We had been to the crematorium earlier in the morning with just family. We then went back to North Breache for drinks and food.

Mother never knew we were leaving North Breache. After the decision was made there were two opportunities when I was about to tell her over a drink in her house but the moment passed each time.

My mother was a wonderful woman. She had won the Irish Ladies Golf Championship in 1926 aged 21. She adored my father who was seventeen years older and who was never very healthy and could be pretty difficult. She nursed him through nearly four years of illness and hideous operations. She was married for only thirty-two years and was a widow for forty-two years. She was physically very tough, down to earth and was universally loved by all who came into contact with her. The loss of my father hit her very hard but she loved North Breache and for many years the farm was an abiding interest.

She always said she could have been a duchess. She became very friendly with the Duke of Grafton and used to go and stay with him. One day, he proposed but she turned him down as she very wisely concluded that he was quite a bit older than her and his family would not have welcomed a new wife.

She always had a black Labrador with which she picked up until she was ninety-seven. When we took over North Breache in 1976 and made a lot of alterations, she never once expressed an opinion even though she undoubtedly felt some of the things we were doing were ridiculous. She was a marvellous cook and into her nineties used to give Pops and me dinner at least once a week.

Having sold North Breache, we had to find somewhere for Rupert and Kerry. They had money from the sale of the lodge. They looked at properties in Somerset and elsewhere but we found a small farm with two substantial bungalows, about forty acres, and a mass of farm buildings and barns. It was about twenty-five minutes from Field House between Frensham and Bordon.

Pops bought one of the houses and an area for a garden around it, and Rupert bought the other house. By this time, Rupert was running a successful contracting business and it was perfect for him as he was able to store the large amount of machinery he acquired in connection with it.

Amanda was a different matter and, sadly, had to leave Eastlands Cottage. Her current man, Ian Sturrock, was not a great favourite of ours but he had a rather scruffy house the other side of Haywards Heath. Although only eleven, the children were all at boarding school and so they moved to Ian's house while they jointly looked to buy something.

They found a house in Thakeham, which suited him so they decided to buy it jointly. There was a major problem with Ian's contribution so Amanda finished up buying the house herself. This was no bad thing as they parted ways within a year.

Will continued to prosper but after their second daughter was born, the marriage was in trouble. They agreed to divorce after failed attempts at reconciliation. It was acrimonious. They had to sell their lovely house on Wandsworth Common, and, eventually, she and Will agreed she should have the equity in the house and he would keep his shares in Lehman. Sadly that was a bad decision as he then left Lehman and they filed for bankruptcy a few months later so his shares were valueless.

Lisa took the young children, Emily and Sophie, to Canada where she met and got remarried to a successful investment banker, John Hockin. They then moved to San Francisco so Will was even further from his children. We then heard the Wilmots must have had problems as they had sold the cottages on Lake Windermere and the house in Florida, which sounded rather sad.

HAMPSHIRE

We moved into Field House on 17 March 2007. We went
and had supper with the Worthingtons at Gaston
Grange. Brett and Anne who had been with us for two years at North
Breache moved with us. Gary and Norleen – she had been a carer for
my mother and Gary worked for me on the farm – elected to stay with
the Farmans where they lived in a mobile home at Eastlands Farm.

Numerous journeys were performed by Gary and Brett to bring
what we wanted from the farm including logs! I had a lot of wine in the
huge cellar at North Breache but no cellar at Field House. Spiral
Cellars dug a deep hole in the back kitchen, which was then fitted out
as a wine cellar with bins sufficient to take 1850 bottles. This was
finished as we moved in.

There was a tennis court in very bad order. On one end, we built a
two-bay garage and a lock-up shed in an oak building. On the other, I
created a vegetable garden with raised beds. The garden was very well
laid out but the shrubberies were overgrown and jungles. Xandra Boyle
put me on to an expert gardener, Brian Green, who agreed to come
and have a look at the garden.

He drove up, got out of his car, introduced himself, and said, 'Most of the gardens I am asked to look at are not worthy of my attention but you have some very nice things here. Can we have a look?'

Brett said he would like to learn more about gardening. Brian ran a school on Saturdays to which Brett went and got seriously hooked on gardening. We also brought back areas of long grass into lawn. We redecorated the house entirely and built a mass of cupboards. We also redid all the carpets. We built a swimming pool in a great spot between tall beech hedge all around.

We caught up with a lot of old friends very quickly as well as new ones, but we were only an hour from all our Surrey and Sussex friends.

I decided to take three days shooting. Hamish Janson gave me a day at Newton Valence. John Russell of Roxtons got me a day at Kirby, which was a lovely shoot on very high ground near Newbury run by Katherine and Richard Astor, and a day at Amesbury on the River Avon. This gave me plenty of shooting. Roddie Petley persuaded me to take a rod on the Kennet at Littlecote, which we did for two or three years before deciding it was too far.

A few years earlier, my cousin Tony (Sir Anthony Nutting) had died. He was always very difficult about offering us a week on the Helmsdale. Some years previously, rather late in the day, he had offered us a week in June. It was Ascot week and we had parties organised and so turned it down. His heir Johnny said we could come whenever we wanted. We started going in October for the stalking, which we all loved. However, we soon graduated to August where we had stags but also two rods on the river.

After a few years, we had settled into life at Field House very well. We had no farm to worry about and the garden was resuscitated if that is the right word and became a pleasure.

Sadly, Brett and Anne decided to emigrate to Australia with one of her sons in New Zealand who had been offered a very good job in Brisbane. They had a great holiday in New Zealand but then the recession and bank crisis of 2008/9 led to the son's job being cancelled and Brett and Anne had no formal qualifications sufficient for a work visa. So, they came back to Scotland where they had a small house and Brett had a brother. Meanwhile, we had hired Phil and Lorraine.

At the party given by the Isdell Carpenters before we arrived, I had got into deep conversation with Hamish Janson who was looking to put together a syndicate to buy a large ocean-going cruising yacht. I was interested and went to look at boats with him, which led us to buying Umatalu. That is a story in itself.

UMATALU

We went with Hamish to inspect a yacht in Southampton. It was being repaired after a fire. We rejected that and some other yachts. Then Hamish found Umatalu in Sardinia. It was not expensive for an 86ft sloop with a great saloon and sleeping accommodation for six and two. It had crew quarters aft, air conditioning, a water maker, and a good engine. Hamish recruited a skipper and his wife. Sea trials were cursory but it seemed good value at 400,000 Euros. We agreed to buy it. Hamish and I each had 25%.

They sailed her from Sardinia to Falmouth where Pops and I joined and sailed up to the Isle of Man where we could pay the VAT and get it straight back. The RYS were having a cruise in Cork and so Hamish and others, now Anthony Balme and Tim Guinness each bought 12.5%. The other 25% was owned by a strange man who Hamish had met on the introduction of Anthony Balme. He had a coal-mining business in Wales, using new techniques to extract coal from slag heaps.

They set sail to Cork but had problems with the engine and the rigging. They put into Dublin and got things going again, missed the RYS in Cork and proceeded back to the Mediterranean. In Corunna, the engine packed up again. We had ordered a new mast and rigging in

La Rochelle. With no engine, the skipper refused to go on and jumped ship. Hamish took his farm manager and recruited three lads off the dock. He then sailed to La Rochelle where he had arranged a berth in a yacht yard.

I was not able to do very much at the time as we were having some problems at Telecom Plus. Hamish then recruited his old Swedish skipper from his previous yacht. Haakon was a fine seaman who brought his own crew of Swedes. Hamish, Lindy, Pops and I drove down to La Rochelle on about six occasions over the next two months or so. We hauled the engine out and drove it back to England to be repaired and then took it back. We put in the new mast and replaced a lot of the rigging. We also overhauled everything else.

I had promised to take the grandchildren, Max, Emma, and Lucy, sailing in Turkey on Umatalu but she was not yet repaired. So, we chartered a 48 ft Beneteau, flew to Turkey and had a wonderful ten days in great heat in August.

Anthony Balme's coal-mining friend had only put up his original £110,000 for his share and had not met any further payments. He now wanted to withdraw. I negotiated a deal with him whereby we released him from further payments provided he left his original contribution in. It was a good deal for us but we needed another 25% investor.

Hamish's close friend Lavinia, married to Charles Perry came in for 12.5% and Jan Matthews who had recently lost his wife and sold his boat came in for 12.5%. We were based in the Mediterranean for the first two years.

Hamish and I, as the major shareholders, had first choice on dates when we wanted to sail for two or three weeks. We had a full-time crew under a skipper so we could move the boat to different places, depending on what the owners wanted. What was remarkable was that in the five years we had Umatalu, there were no problems about who had her and when. We sometimes sailed with other partners and sometimes we took friends and or family.

We had a dreadful trip from Palma, planning to go to Sicily. It was Pops and me, David and Angela Darling, and John Ingledew. Haakon failed to get a proper weather forecast. We had a lovely sail to the south of Minorca when the wind and rain got up. In the event, we had a full force-nine gale for forty-two hours with only a storm jib. I spent most of the time on the wheel. Instead of Sicily, we finished up at Alghero not far from the north of Sardinia. At one stage, David Darling failed to put on his leeboards and flew out of his cabin, through the passage and into John Ingledew's cabin landing on top of him.

I tried to stop glasses coming out of the fiddles in the saloon. I lurched against the large fixed table that came adrift and with me under it, crashed across the cabin. Miraculously, I was unhurt. We then went to Corsica and the delightful harbour of Bonifacio.

From there, we sailed for Rome where we found we drew too much to get into the main marina and harbour at Ostia despite all information that we could easily do so. We had to sail up the coast to Linaro where there was a marina we could enter. There, our voyage ended. Later we came out and others sailed down to Sicily. We flew to Catania in Sicily, which was a horrible place with no public services working as workers were long unpaid. We hired a car, got a bit lost and three thugs threw a bicycle in front of us, climbed on the car and tried to open the doors. I managed to nearly avoid the bike, swerved, and drove away at speed. The chap on the bonnet must have been badly hurt and the bike damaged.

We stayed for two nights in the hotel where we had stayed after Will was born. The Villa San Andrea owned by Dicky and Jane Manley in those days was unrecognisable. It had been built up all around but Taormina was still a fun place with the funicular still working from Taormina on Sea.

We had a nice lunch and then drove north to a little fishing port where Umatalu and Haakon were. We were with Rupert and Kerry, and Amanda and the boyfriend Ian. We went around all the islands, including Stromboli and sailed down to Catania from where we flew home. Kerry was a bit sick. Ian was really bad company, going ashore and getting drunk. He left early with some excuse about business. Amanda immediately fell in love with Haakon.

The crew then took her to Turkey where other partners enjoyed trouble -sailing. We went out again with Charlie and Mel Petre, and David and Angela. We sailed from Bodrum down to nearly Antalya. It was very hot and humid, at about 45 C. The coal-mining ex-partner then chartered her to go to Northern Cyprus where his wife, who came from a very rich and influential Turkish family, had significant interests. Amanda went as crew.

Tim Guinness then took her back to Palma via Crete where she was prepared for the Atlantic crossing. Anthony Balme was going to do the ARK transatlantic race but pulled out at the last minute so Haakon and crew took her across the Atlantic. A week before Christmas, we flew to Antigua and chartered two small aeroplanes to fly us to St Maarten. We joined Umatalu there with Amanda and Max, Emma, and Lucy.

We sailed to Anguilla, St Barts and then to Antigua where we were joined by Max and Elisabeth Neilson in English Harbour where we had Christmas day. Our Swedish crew cooked a Swedish Christmas dinner, which no one much fancied. Next, we spent a day in Dominica. There were a few more buildings but not much had changed. We went into Shillingford's, which seemed very busy. I spoke on the telephone to Julius Timothy who could not meet us as he was Minister for Trade and was very busy with meetings. We went up to the Boiling Lake and the freshwater lake to which there was now an adequate road.

We finished in St Lucia where Anthony Balme picked her up and sailed down to Grenada. Haakon brought her on to Venezuela. At the end of January, we flew to Caracas and spent a night in a hotel. It was a horrible place, and very dangerous. The next day, there were problems at the airport with our tickets. I had to pay again and was dealt with by very officious airport people.

We had the Spring Rices with us and Pop's sister Tinky and husband Chris. Eventually, we got our small aeroplane flight to Los Rocos islands. We had two weeks there. It was a nice little town. To fly back, we had to pay again for our flights but only in local currency. We all rushed around the town gathering together what we could and eventually had enough. We did some bonefishing, which was fun. They were lovely islands and we had a lovely relaxing time there. Umatalu required some things doing to her and so Haakon and the crew took her to Cartagena where there was a good yacht yard.

Some three weeks later, I flew out to Cartagena in Colombia by myself via Bogota. Hamish, Lindy and the Perrys were already there. We had hoped to sail on but there was a week's delay waiting for a spare part to arrive. There was a very attractive old town with a lot of history and so it was not too great a penance to spend some days there. They had found quite a nice little hotel where we stayed. Eventually, we were able to sail and went to the San Blas Islands just off Merrien in Panama where that ill-fated settlement of Scots perished 200 years ago. On the mainland, there was dense jungle rising up steeply. There were tiny little islands that were densely populated. The men fished and the women embroidered. It was part of Panama but independent.

We then sailed on to Panama and the canal at Colon, aptly named. We had to wait for passage through the canal. We were then roped up with a smaller yacht on each side of us. We got into the canal in the late afternoon and then through three locks. It was huge enough to take a small cruise liner. The engines on the underground cables manoeuvre everything. We had a pilot on board who we'd had to wait for before entering the canal. It is mightily impressive and it was evident they were building and excavating so they could widen it.

We came into a large lake that comprised much of the journey before two locks down to the Pacific. Panama City is on the Pacific. It was a busy place with a nice old city.

We sailed out to the Las Perlas Islands and spent two days there doing a bit of diving and swimming. This is where the Shah of Persia holed up when he was deposed. We sailed back to Panama.

Tim and Beverley Guinness had joined the party to go to Gala-pagos and on to the Marquesas. Having already been to Galapagos, I stood down for this trip and, after a few days, I flew back home. They had only a short time in Galapagos due to restrictions on visiting yachts. They then put up a spinnaker and set sail for the Marquesas doing 2800 miles in eleven days. The spinnaker was put down on arrival in the Marquesas.

A considerable atmosphere had been developing between Hamish who was the managing partner and Haakon so, on arrival there, it was agreed Haakon should leave with his crew on arrival in Tahiti. He always wanted an only Swedish crew chosen by him. We had also found out in Panama that Haakon and his friends owned a Jeanneau 40, which was following us. This provided a ready source of crew for us but there had clearly been some confusion over what stores were for us or what for Haakon's boat. It had been an unsatisfactory arrangement for some time together with Haakon's unwillingness to get his hands dirty on maintenance rather than directing his crew.

In Cartagena, we had hired an English girl as a cook as the previous Swedish cook had left and Haakon had no ready replacement. She was a brilliant girl who was not only an excellent cook but very good on deck and attractive. Haakon was not happy and made her life difficult so she left in Panama. Very cleverly, Hamish had been in contact with, and on arrival in Tahiti met up with, Matthieu Volueur. He was French, only twenty-nine but very familiar with the Pacific Islands.

He was a breath of fresh air and soon became a good friend. He brought with him a delightful girlfriend, Zori, who was Bulgarian, was excellent on deck, did the cabins, and served drinks. He had a Brazilian as engineer and we kept the Swedish cook. That was the set up when we flew to Tahiti via LA. We spent three nights in LA on the way and revisited the Beverley Hills Hotel. We had a car and went down to Santa Monica. On arrival, we spent two nights in a hotel in Papeete while Matthieu and team got the boat ready.

We were joined by Loudie and Elisabeth Constantine and John and Anna Ingledew. We sailed to Moorea where we swam with Rays and then on down the Society Islands to Bora Bora. Ta'aha was particularly nice and Matthieu and I visited a family who had a farm. We brought back a mass of fruit.

We got the dive setup going as Matthieu was very keen. Using the tender, we went out beyond the reefs surrounding all the islands and went over the side into a mass of big and small fish. There was anything up to fifty sharks in view at any time; there were white tips, black tips, grey sharks, and lemon sharks. There were also lots of barracuda in packs of fifty or more.

At night, we anchored inside the reefs but it was always quite windy, which provided a current. I was very happy swimming around with a mask and flippers but no one else was very keen on swimming, which was a pity.

Having got to the last Society Island furthest from Tahiti we then had to get back. Strong winds and rough seas were forecast and so the girls, Pops, Anna and Elisabeth flew from Bora Bora to Tahiti and us boys took the boat back to Moorea where we decided to spend a few days while Matthieu took the boat to Papeete and readied it for our trip to the Tuamoto Archipelago about 200 miles north.

We stayed in a delightful hotel for a few nights and where Pops bought some wonderful black pearls. The Darlings came and joined us there. We then took the ferry back to Papeete with all our luggage. David had his passport in a small bag that disappeared at some stage on the ferry trip, including his cash but not his credit cards. More about that later.

The Constantines and Ingledews left us with just the Darlings.

We sailed up to Rangiroa in the Tuamotos, which was a huge lagoon some forty-five miles across with lots of little islands in a circle. Matthieu had a friend who ran a small dive school. Business was pretty slow so she was happy to lend us large tanks and take us in her big rib out beyond the reef in big seas. I did five dives with her and Matthieu, which were each sensational drift dives with us going at about 5 knots at times. There were amazing fish. We caught quite a few tuna, which we filleted and feasted on.

Our voyage back to Tahiti was windy with rain and not very comfortable. We said goodbye to Matthieu and the crew who set off west where Jan Matthews was picking the boat up. We then flew home, having had a sensational time.

We next caught up with Umatalu in February in Auckland, New Zealand with Hamish, Lindy, Anthony Balme and Mary Lou, and Tim and Beverley Guinness. We cruised up to the Bay of Islands and further north and then back to Auckland. The sea was quite cold and the only decent dive site was infested with nasty, small jellyfish.

Before that, Pops and I had flown into Auckland, hired a car and driven around the North Island. We met up with David Langdale who was married to Jane Glass who I had known sailing in Cowes. He had been very prominent in hunting, which was conducted exactly as in the UK but the quarry was hares. They were broke and in a very small house. We took them out to dinner and then went to Wellington where we met up with Rod and Glennis Smith. He was writing a history of the Guinness family in NZ and Australia and had come to see us at Field House.

We then flew to Christchurch, hired another car, and did the South Island, Christchurch, Mt Cook and then four days in Queenstown.

Christchurch was beautiful with a stunning botanical garden. We visited the cathedral there where there was a flower festival. Two days later, we were in Queenstown Airport when the second Christchurch earthquake occurred, which we felt and which collapsed the cathedral. We also visited a friend of Amanda's who showed us the lovely house they had just built on to. It was on a hillside overlooking the sea. Following the earthquake, it slid down the hillside and all was lost. New Zealand was lovely but quite boring. There were no cars anywhere except Auckland.

In Auckland, we had Umatalu slipped and it was apparent the keel was in bad order. A new one was a minimum of £350,000 and we all agreed we should sell her. We went back home via Bali and Singapore. In the former, we stayed with the Orchards and then spent a lovely week in Sumbawa where I did some diving with wonderful coral but not many big fish.

In Singapore, we did lots of shopping and then headed home as we had been away for nearly seven weeks.

Umatalu failed to sell in Auckland and so the crew took her to Brisbane where we put her in an auction and she sold for about $100,000.

On our return, David Darling was still in Tahiti as he had masses of problems getting anyone to replace his passport or an airline to fly him back. There was no British consulate in Tahiti. Eventually, Air New

Zealand flew him via Auckland, Singapore, Tokyo and back to London where immigration were very loath to admit him without a passport. Angela went to the airport and eventually persuaded them not to send him back to New Zealand or Tahiti.

That was the end of Umatalu.

BENTWORTH

$\mathcal{O}$ur first four or five years at Bentworth were taken up with sailing on Umatalu and initially getting the garden straight. I found myself doing less and less work. By 2012, I had retired from Telecom Plus and Hampden Agencies. In my late seventies, I was reluctant to take on new commitments.

Amanda had a new man in her life, David Ferguson alias Fergie. Older than her by eight years, he had no job, and no money but turned out to be a decent and kind person. Will found and bought a wonderful house just over Battersea Bridge. Rupert went from strength to strength with his contracting business and had some sheep, pigs, and cattle as well as chickens. He also had a small horse livery business and Kerry had a horse and a pony.

In 2011, I went to Russia to the Rynda River near Murmansk with a large party with Derek Strauss, Mark Cannon Brooks, and others. It was all helicopters, comfortable lodge, and good food but the fishing was difficult. It involved wading up to my chest in fast-flowing icy water with rocks. I decided I was ten years too late but it was a wonderful fun experience.

In 2012, we got Brett and Anne back. We went to fish on the Oykel when we heard from Phil that he and Lorraine were giving us notice as they were leaving in thirty days' time as per their contract. This was within the time they knew we had taken a house near Aix for two weeks. I asked whether they could stay on for a few more days to cover our return. They declined.

We felt we had to return south and, on the way down, Pops contacted Anne Jackman to ascertain whether she had any ideas. She promptly said, 'What about us?'

We told Phil and Lorraine to leave within days and said we would not provide any references. The new job near Winchester did not work out and they left within ten days. They had been reliable and we had no real doubts about their trustworthiness but he was a barrack-room lawyer, a clock watcher and I supposed we had not ever really liked him.

It was a great relief to have Anne and Brett back. Also, the holiday went well. We had all Will's children and Amanda's, and the Armitages and Darlings in a fine house with a lovely pool.

I continued to play a lot of golf for Boodles' and the Guards.

In July 2012, I took Max off to America to look at American Universities. We stayed with friends of Will's near Boston and saw four universities there. We then flew to Washington, stayed at the Metropolitan Club, and saw three universities there plus a train journey to Philadelphia to hire a car and go to LeHigh at Bethlehem. It was a lovely campus but Bethlehem was the rust capital of USA. Bethlehem Steel had been the largest producer in the world and the massive, rusty, abandoned works dominated the skyline.

In November, we went to a showcase of US universities in Kensington town hall and added Richmond to our list. Max applied to about ten universities who all offered him a place. In April, Pops and I went with Max to make a choice. We went to two in the Boston area and American University in Washington, and then Richmond. It was a no-brainer with a lovely campus, really nice people, and Richmond was a great city. In August, we went back but with Amanda and moved Max into his room at the University of Richmond.

In 2013, we decided to have a party in July and had about 175 people to *eats on your feet*. This was an event done by Jane Holmes who is a super caterer and who with a previous husband had built Field House some twenty-five years previously before selling to the Isdell Carpenters. It was a huge success and we were lucky to have a fine day. We mixed Hampshire with Surrey, Sussex, and London.

My vegetable garden became great fun. It was on the old tennis court, which had been in a terrible condition when we'd bought the place. We also planted a lot of fruit and this kept me busy in the summer and the vegetable garden all year.

We had no Umatalu and so we were able to plan lovely winter holidays including Soneva Fushi in the Maldives, Soneva Kiri, and a six-senses resort in Thailand. We spent a week with Brian Trafford in his wonderful house south-east of Nairobi and then flew to Johannesburg and then to the Wankie Game reserve in Zimbabwe. We took another flight to Victoria Falls where we were amazed to find the grand hotel of that name in Zimbabwe still had the old pictures of British royalty where they had always been. We did two reserves in Botswana in one of which we rode on African elephants. Finally, via Johannesburg, we flew up to Pemba in Northern Mozambique and then to an island offshore, Azura Qualalia.

While still at North Breache, we had started to become keen on opera and went to the Coliseum and Covent Garden with friends. We also went to the Grange in Hampshire and then found it was less than fifteen minutes from Field House. By this time, we regularly went to Covent Garden as well. We took a party to most things done at the Grange.

In 2016, Wasfi Kani who had created Grange Park Opera failed rather acrimoniously to agree on a new lease when it came up for renewal. She desperately needed a new home and was introduced to Bamber Gascoigne who had inherited West Horsley Place in Surrey. She persuaded him to give Grange Park Opera a ninety-nine-year lease and set about raising the money – some £13 million in total – to build a new opera house.

We had become fond of and admirers of Wasfi and became founders. I was lucky to have quite a lot of money in my charitable trust and handily, opera companies are charities. Since then, we have become very friendly with Wasfi and have taken a party to nearly everything they have done there. As founders, we get to go backstage after the performance with our party, which is great fun. However, we have continued to patronise the local Grange Festival at the Grange. It's all rather confusing but it continues well under new direction. We also still go up to Covent Garden.

Again, in about 2014, we were asked by Carolyn Townsend whether we would like to become fellows of the RHS. This means again, getting your cheque book out but again a charity in part. We get tickets to the Chelsea Flower Show on the Monday preview day and an invitation to lunch. There were also fellows' trips to famous gardens and abroad, a dinner in London, and a summer party as well as visits to Wisley. We have been to Italy and America and some wonderful gardens here. We found many of the keen fellows on these trips, who are normally limited to twenty-four or thirty, became or were good friends already.

In 2015, I was going to be eighty and we had already been married for fifty years so we had a lunch party for 220 friends in a tent on our lawn. The most difficult thing was the seating plan for 220 people at tables of ten. We had plentiful eats as a first course and then sat them down and served fish and chips. A feature was a chocolate fountain into which you dipped strawberries and cake. As people left it was noticeable that many of the men in their smart white coats had liberal amounts of chocolate down their fronts. Will gave a very good short speech. I am so lucky that Pops is the most wonderful organiser of a party with amazing attention to detail.

A sad but too frequent occurrence was the death of friends. First, while just still at North Breache was Oliver Chesterton, my uncle. I was rather surprised by his elder son, Mike, asking me to do the tribute at the funeral service. That was my first. Next was Michael Boyle who had a small burial service and then a huge memorial service in Winchester Cathedral. He was a great Hampshire and sailing character and there was a full cathedral, about 1000 people. There was so much to say about such a wonderful character that I think I took nearly twenty minutes. You have to speak slowly in a cathedral as I learned in Guildford when High Sheriff. Soon afterwards, Jeremy Durham Matthews died in Wincanton. I had, of course, shared that first very grand flat with him and Michael Boyle. They had a lovely service in Wincanton and I paid tribute to Jeremy, which was not so easy as he had had a rather chequered business career.

Then Charlie Petre in the Catholic Church in Hook. Next was an old girlfriend of many years ago who had become a very sad character, Jennie Carnegie. The family were very sweet but it was in a tiny church north of Andover. If that was not enough my old friend with whom I had messed at Eton, Simon Horn died in London with a very full Chelsea Old Church. After a bit of discussion about who should do the tribute, I found myself doing it.

Then there was our very old friend Tony Boyden, a great sailor and friend. There had been a few problems with the private funeral and Tony was a Christian Scientist so Caroline decided to have a drinks party at the Royal Thames in London to celebrate Tony's life. She asked me to stand up and say a few words so this in a way was another memorial service. He was a great man and a very good friend.

One of the joys of getting older has been to appreciate how lucky we have been with our children. Two divorces out of three has been sad but a better average than the Queen! Amanda is running a successful B&B business and comes to see us a lot. In 2013, Rupert and Kerry had a son out of the blue with Kerry aged forty-six. We see a lot of them as they are not far away. In 2014, we had a bit of a shock when Rupert was rushed into hospital with a ruptured gut. He had to have a series of operations, including the loss of a kidney. He made a wonderful recovery and runs his very successful contracting business doing a lot of heavy work himself. Will then followed two years later when he was sailing with his friend Tara Getty and they were run down by a larger yacht. Will got squashed and broke a number of ribs and punctured a lung. He was in hospital in St Tropez for ten days. We flew down and Pops stayed with him but I had to return. I then drove down and we brought him back only for him then to have to spend a week in the John Radcliffe in Oxford. He has also made a good recovery and keeps in close touch but has a very busy life. Then we are so lucky with Amanda's children. Max did so well at university in Richmond, Virginia, where he got a wonderful education. He is the nicest person you could wish for and I think he will be very successful. I have always regarded myself as a sort of surrogate father to him. He is currently working in Kenya and I think he will be destined to make his way abroad. Emma and Lucy are wonderful to their grandparents and come and see us frequently. They have a huge circle of friends and are such fun. All three of them have a very strong work ethic and good jobs.

Will's daughters have done well at their schools in America. Emily is in her last year at her boarding school near Santa Barbara, Dunn, where she is very popular, articulate, and sporty and has emerged as a bit of a leader among her peers. She is also very pretty and seems much admired by the boys! Sophie is quite different. She is very hard working and academic and has learned Mandarin from an early age. She is also a very fine tennis player and plays soccer for a South California team. Like her sister she is also very self-assured and pretty. Sadly, Will's relationship with Lisa remains very difficult, which is not helpful to the girls seeing enough of their father or he of them.

In 2018, we decided we would put a lake in at the bottom of our garden where it lay rather wet. This was 750 sq. metres in area and was finished at the end of October. It was too late to sow grass seed and so we turfed a very large area. No soil was taken away so we changed the contours of the big lawn. It filled from rainwater and we had a number of problems with leaks around the area in the liner where the surface rainwater came into the lake. As I write, we hope we have cured the problem. The lake has hugely enhanced the whole garden and we have had a lot of fun planting shrubs.

In February 2020, we took much of the family to Kenya. Max was working there. Pops and I spent three nights in the Muthaiga Club, which had not changed much although Nairobi certainly was a very much bigger city than one remembered.

We then met up with Charlie, Rupert's eldest, Emma and Lucy, and went to Richards Camp in the Mara for four days where we saw everything except leopard Then we flew up to Sarara, between Mt Kenya and Lake Rudolf. It was very different and Max joined us there. We then went back to Nairobi where we met up with Amanda and Fergie. Max left us to go back to work and Charlie had to return to school. We then flew down to Kalifi on the coast where Annabelle, our tour organiser, had found us quite the nicest house you could imagine. Max came down for a week and Nicki Ropner spent three days with us. After twelve days, it was time to return home. Ten days later lockdown was imposed for Covid-19. Max was sent back from Kenya a week later.

As my eighty-fifth birthday is imminent, it seems a suitable time to finish this book, although I hope to live for many more years yet.

As I write, we are, due to Covid 19, living under draconian rules and regulations, all backed up by law, which I could never have dreamed could happen in this country. Those people running the country are terrified of getting it wrong. My worry is the harm being done to those with cancer, heart disease and, in particular, suffering from a mental illness whose treatment is postponed or cancelled because of the virus. We know so much more about it so nearly everyone, even the very old, recover.

I hazard a guess that many more people will die from lack of treatment of routine cancers, heart and lung problems, and mental illness leading to suicides. We are in a mess.

Made in the USA
Monee, IL
24 September 2021